catching fireflies

catching fireflies

TEACHING YOUR HEART TO SEE
GOD'S LIGHT EVERYWHERE

PATSY CLAIRMONT

THOMAS NELSON
Since 1798

NASHVILLE DALLAS MEXICO CITY RIO DE JANEIRO BEIJING

Catching Fireflies

© 2009 by Patsy Clairmont

All rights reserved. No portion of this book may be reproduced, stored in
a retrieval system, or transmitted in any form or by any means—
electronic, mechanical, photocopy, recording, or any other—except for
brief quotation in printed reviews, without the prior written permission
of the publisher.

Published in Nashville, Tennessee. Thomas Nelson is a registered
trademark of Thomas Nelson, Inc.

Thomas Nelson, Inc. titles may be purchased in bulk for educational,
business, fund-raising, or sales promotional use. For information, please
e-mail SpecialMarkets@ThomasNelson.com.

Unless otherwise noted, Scripture quotations are taken from New
American Standard Bible, © 1960, 1977, 1995 by the Lockman Foundation.
Used by permission.

Scriptures noted NIV are taken from *The Holy Bible, New International
Version* © 1973, 1978, 1984 by International Bible Society. Used by
permission of Zondervan Publishing House.

Scriptures noted KJV are taken from the King James Version of the Bible.
Public domain.

An effort has been made to locate sources and obtain permission where
necessary for the quotations used in this book. In the event of any
unintentional omission, a modification will gladly be incorporated in
future printings.

Library of Congress Cataloging-in-Publication Data

Clairmont, Patsy.
  Catching fireflies : teaching your heart to see God's light everywhere
/ Patsy Clairmont.
     p. cm.
  ISBN 978-1-4002-0238-6
  1. Christian women--Religious life. 2. Light--Religious
aspects--Christianity. I. Title.
  BV4527.C5327 2009
  248.8'43--dc22

2008044838

Printed in the United States of America

09 10 11 12 13 QW 9 8

❀

To a "firefly" of extraordinary brilliance . . .
Ellie Lofaro

contents

contents

one

In the Beginning

I'm a light girl. No, not low tonnage. I wish.

What I love is illumination—morning sunrays sneaking around the corners of my window shades, encouraging me to rise up; the yellow glow on a firefly's keister dancing in the distance; or lightning streaking across a night sky like an insistent exclamation point. If it lights up, I like it. With the exception of red bubbles on top of police cars beckoning me to chat. Quite honestly, I just don't have the time.

I

I'm sure my fascination with light-bearing objects is why I love the book of Genesis, especially the part where light was birthed.

When God said, "Let there be light," there was! But take note that He didn't design the light holders —the sun, moon, and stars—until four days later. Have you ever considered that, during creation, light was bounding about willy-nilly until it was corralled into designated positions? That fascinates me. I wonder if it looked like an explosive aurora borealis.

I would have loved a front row seat for that light show. I think.

Then again, in Scripture, people responded by falling on their faces when they encountered a heavenly messenger, witnessed a miracle, or heard God's voice. They had a compelling reason for responding that way, I'm sure. We humans derive a great deal of our security from what we know, and generally speaking, we're not sturdy enough for the "other world," full of its wondrously fierce mysteries.

Remember when Moses climbed to the mountaintop and asked to see God? The Lord's mercy covered Moses as He passed by because Moses wasn't prepared for what he would have seen. Oh, he might have been desirous, curious, and even devotion-driven to look on the Lord, but God knew Moses wasn't ready for such a startling encounter.

Majesty, purity, and holiness, to name a few of God's qualities, are piercing in their perfect state. Our hearts couldn't take the jolt.

Remember Jacob? He wrestled with an angel, and because of that encounter, he walked with a limp the rest of his life.

When angels appeared to people, the heavenly beings greeted those mere mortals with the words, "Fear not." They understood that fear would be our first, knee-knocking response.

So taking into consideration that we wouldn't have had the moxie to handle witnessing the first stirrings in the universe, let's stretch our limited minds and try to imagine it. A time when there was no time (what must that be like?), just total darkness (now I'm scared), chaos (this feels familiar), and emptiness (I don't do bottomless falls).

Actually, reading that description—dark, chaotic, and empty—reminds me of last week, when my son's visiting Jack Russell discovered our laundry basket full of clean clothes. He chewed the support out of my new underwire. I am of the personal belief that Jack Russells were fashioned from the spare parts of pogo sticks. No, I'm not bitter, just reflecting on how, perhaps, this Jack Russell's interior must resemble creation before God brought order to it.

Alas, I digress. Back to the invention of light.

Let's consider for a moment what happens when the universe's scary dark is abruptly interrupted. At God's command, light crashes through utter darkness, bursting forth as conqueror.

Does that sound superhero-ish? Well, that's my interpretation of how it might have happened. And whether light crashed onto the scene, sauntered in, or flowed like a river, we know this for sure: God spoke, and it was so! Which should be a strong reminder for us about the wallop God's words carry.

Recently I was thinking about the phrase, "Let there be light," and it hit me anew that those are

God's first recorded words. I don't know if that makes them more important or holier than anything else He said, but that reminder caused me to lean in and listen deeply because I don't want to miss the impact of His proclamations.

As I further explored "Let there be light," I was reminded that not only does Scripture's first book open with light, but the last book also closes with it. The theme throughout the Bible, from beginning to end, cover to cover, from Genesis to Revelation, is Jesus, the Light of the World.

As a matter of fact, we could say that the Bible is bookended in light *and* a holy fire. For light is the symbol God has chosen to represent truth, and Jesus is the flame of our faith. Of course, divine insight is full of light, and Christ is that light; so anytime we understand something that's true, something we never had grasped before, Jesus is all over it. Don't you love that?

I can become downright giddy when a fresh truth settles inside me. I want to shout from the rooftop, "I get it! I get it! I finally get it!"

I've found "in the beginning" truth igniting. It sparks hope inside me, whether it's the beginning of a grand new day, a new project, a new resolution, or a new understanding.

I hope this book will offer you new understandings and thoughts that kindle your desire to seek God in fresh ways. Together we will explore different kinds of illumination that help us to find that path. I've been known to lose my way, and I've been ever so grateful to those who have come alongside me with their lanterns to shed some light on the direction to take. So if you're feeling unsure, take my hand, and we'll step this out together. I believe that just as surely as God had a place assigned for the sun, moon, and stars, He has a place for us as His light holders. A place where we get to shine.

I hope, shiny girlfriends, we can take time for some laughter, too, for it will lighten our load and our countenances. My prayer is that you might find in this book God-inspired bright ideas to slip into your purse to help clarify your next step, and the next, and the one after that . . . even in the dark.

two

Fireflies

His sanguine spirit turns every firefly into a star.

—Arthur Conan Doyle Sr.

I love when my dreams are of steamy summer nights dripping in hand-cranked ice cream. Then that yummy dream is drizzled with squealing children who fill mason jars with fireflies. That's my remembrance of childhood summer vacations.

More than fifty years ago I was one of those squealers, and when I think about it, I still can feel the same tummy-giggle at the sight of the lightning bugs that dotted the landscape with magic. Those pinpoint flashes sent us kids dashing down the hill to capture them in our glass jars. Then we would line up the jars on the picnic table, creating a row of luminous lanterns. Oh, how they glowed!

Today Michigan, my home state, has lightning bugs aplenty on the edges of our woods, pleasing me with wisps of promise. But long ago and far away, the fireflies of Kentucky won my childhood favor. Fireflies are a child's white lightning, leaving us tipsy with glee.

I remember how, after I had eaten a heaping bowl of homemade ice cream, I would carry my treasured firefly jar, pinging with fireflies, into my mamaw's home to get ready for bed. After my bath, I would climb into shorty pajamas and crawl between the sun-sweet sheets onto a feather bed. The whirring of the nearby fan created a rhythmic lullaby, sending ripples of cool air across my pillow. When I sank into the pinstriped covering of the down bedding, it would rise up around me to form puffy clouds. My last waking moments were a delicious blend of adult voices drifting on the breeze and my nearby jar still abuzz with specks of light.

By morning my lively lantern light would be

gone, the jar carried to the front porch after I fell asleep and my light bearers freed. The empty jar sat next to my papaw's rocker awaiting another night run. I wouldn't disappoint it. As darkness settled around the house, I would once again run, capture light, have more ice cream, and then sink into dreamland.

Dreams are prevalent throughout Scripture. Firefly dreams? Not so much. But the Bible's dreams or visions always seem to contain light, whether a burning bush (Exodus 3); Paul's Damascus road encounter (Acts 9); Joseph's dream in which the sun, the moon, and eleven stars bowed down to him (Genesis 37); or Daniel's dream about the Ancient of Days sitting on a throne blazing in fire (Daniel 7). Why, Scripture's "dream" scenes are flooded with light, when you think about it.

So we shouldn't be surprised when dreams bring enlightenment—if not to us, then maybe to others. Like what happened to me one morning a few months ago . . .

During the first thirty minutes I'm awake, I'm

not an eager participant in the morning, and then I get over myself and move on into the day. This particular morning I hadn't yet shaken the webs of sleep loose when my husband Les came in, holding out the phone to me. I had heard it ring but had ignored it. I shook my head to indicate that I didn't want to talk yet. I hadn't yet brushed my teeth, and I don't talk until after I brush. It's in the world's best interest. Les gave me a look that strongly suggested I speak into the phone. So I did . . . with a snarl.

Then what I heard on the other end changed everything. A woman whose lips dripped Southern accent said, "Is this Patsy Clairmont?"

All my kin were from Kentucky, but those whom I knew and loved there have gone to be with Jesus. So when I heard the lilt of her voice, drenched in sweet tea, she became my new best friend and a postcard from heaven. My head buzzed with fireflies.

"You are going to think I'm crazy," she continued, "but I had a dream. I dreamed that I was talking to a woman on the telephone, and she asked me, 'Do you have a list of potential friends?'

"I told her, 'No, I don't. Who is this?'

"'This is Patsy Clairmont,' she answered."

And then the woman who had called me said she woke up.

"I thought it was a strange dream, and it made no sense to me," the Southern voice confessed. "But it wouldn't leave me. It followed me from one room to another. Finally I did what I always do when I'm not sure what to do: I got down on my knees, and I prayed. I said, 'Lord, this dream makes no sense to me. So if You are trying to tell me something, I don't understand.'"

That was when she heard a voice within her, which she knew to be the Lord's, say, *I want you to tell Patsy Clairmont that I have not forgotten her.*

"I'm willing to do that, Lord, but who is Patsy Clairmont?"

Silence.

The Southern phone voice continued, "I went on with my life, but His instruction remained clear in the back of my mind that I was to call someone I didn't know. I took a trip, came back home, and was busy restoring order to my home, when I pulled a book off my library shelf. It was a book I had never read, and I was trying to decide if I should keep it or pass it on. A friend had given it to me when I had my first grandchild, and now I have five, and I still hadn't gotten around to reading it. It was a compilation book, and I glanced down at the authors listed on the cover. That's when I saw the name Patsy Clairmont."

She made a series of calls and was able to track down my number. "I'm not a sweating woman," she confessed, "but my hands were perspiring when I dialed your number. I asked the Lord, 'Couldn't You give me something more significant to say than You have not forgotten her?'"

I had listened intently to her dream, her prayer, and now her concern. "You know what?" I said. "I don't think you could have told me anything more moving and significant than that God has not forgotten me. That He would put my name in your dream and a message in your heart, and that you would have the courage to follow through so I might be encouraged is deeply touching."

After we hung up (and I brushed my teeth), I was basking in the wonder of God's love. And then I remembered . . . in the wee hours of the night I had awakened, slipped out of bed, and curled into a chair in my office to study and pray. I had asked the Lord if He would clarify the message He wanted me to speak to women this year, but the heavens seemed still. After a time of waiting, I crawled back in bed and slept soundly until I awoke again.

As I pondered the sequence of my hours, I realized that the message the woman delivered was not only for me personally but also the answer to my prayer for the women I would encounter this year. "God has not forgotten you" was to be the heartbeat of my message, the lantern lit with God's love.

My friend, God has not forgotten you. He knows your sorrow, your troubles, your finances, your fears, and your dreams—and He has not forgotten you. He promises to redeem our hardships for our good. Sometimes we think that if God doesn't fix or change our struggles, then He must have forgotten us. Nothing could be further from the truth.

Questions to Ask Yourself

❀ Did your childhood sparkle with fireflies? If not, what creatures lit up your life?

❀ What important dreams have you had?

❀ Do you have trouble getting over yourself? In what areas?

❀ What do you tend to do when you don't know what to do?

❀ When have the heavens seemed silent to you?

Bright Ideas

Consider Job. People have been for centuries. Job lost everything that mattered to him except his wife. And as if that wasn't enough, he was covered in oozing sores. His wife thought he should curse God and die. That was her only recorded contribution. Sad, but understandable coming from a woman who had just buried all her children. She had given up, thrown in the proverbial towel. We hear it in her grief-torn, anger-laden words.

Job hung on even when friends arrived and said all the wrong things. Just when Job needed them the most, their counsel only added to his indignities. But then Job began to see past his pain, past the people, and past opinions, to flickers of light in the dark night of his soul. He heard God speak, and the Lord's every word glowed with a future.

Job entered the lantern-lined path of hope. His life-picture shifted, and his end years flourished.

"The LORD blessed the latter days of Job more than his beginning" (Job 42:12).

A life of faith involves seeing past what's happening today and believing in God's redemptive care in our tomorrows. How do we respond like Job? Let's see . . . Job didn't run around frantic (my tendency); he sat down and listened (not so much my tendency); he didn't give up even in the face of despair (hmm); he knew God's voice (I like that); and he leaned into God's sovereignty (my life goal).

"I know that You can do all things, and that no purpose of Yours can be thwarted" (Job 42:2).

1. Be still
2. Listen
3. Believe
4. Discern
5. Accept

Five luminous lanterns to help us during our night-seasons to know God hasn't forgotten us. Be attentive when it's the darkest, for that's when lightning bugs do their best work . . . and nothing fans faith's imagination like the dance of a firefly!

❋

To accomplish great things, we must not only act,
but also dream; not only plan, but also believe.

—ANATOLE FRANCE

three

Morning Light

> *The windows of my soul I throw wide open to the sun.*
>
> —JOHN GREENLEAF WHITTIER

Have you ever noticed how invigorating dawn light skipping across wooden floors is? Or the wonder of morning light as it refracts off prisms, twirling rainbows on ceilings? Even though I'm not naturally an early bird, I confess I'm disappointed when I miss those first soft rays that fill the morning with light. That's when dew sparkles like a bride's diamond, tulips rouse full, tomatoes glisten on windowsills, and droplets of light freckle my bedroom wall.

No wonder photographers stir before sunrise and wait expectantly for daybreak's dance to waltz past their lenses. It's spectacular, warm, hopeful, dimensional, promising, and artistic.

On toasty summer mornings, my favorite spot is a garden. In those early hours, joy blooms in pots, runs askew down pansy borders, stretches up sunflower walls, and is fence-festive in morning glories. Call me an intruder, but I love to carry my camera to a patch of veronica and slip up on a butterfly sipping nectar or a grasshopper nibbling a leaf. "Breakfast," I hear the nearby bumblebee buzz.

Morning births opportunities. I like that. Because some days become sullied, and I find it encouraging to know that, within hours, a new day will unfold with a potential fresh start.

Yesterday was sullied for my son, Jason, and his wife, Danya. Oh, nothing they won't recover from, just one of those bee-stinging days during which you wonder, "What else could go wrong?" Then, sure enough, something else does.

Jason and Danya, by dawn's early light, were packing to drive from Daytona Beach to Jacksonville, Florida, to catch a flight to Michigan.

They had grabbed a few days of vacation, and now they were headed home to their two eager sons. About halfway to the airport, they received a call from the airline that their flight had been cancelled. So they shifted to plan B, and when they reached the airport, they booked another flight. No big deal.

The new flight wasn't direct like their original, but it would get them home. But, for some reason, when the reservation desk personnel printed out the boarding passes for the connecting flight in New York, Jason's wouldn't print. So he was told he would have to pick up the pass for the second leg of their journey after he arrived in New York. Inconvenient, but tolerable.

After they touched down at LaGuardia, they had to wait for a bus to change terminals, but when they arrived, because Jason had no boarding pass, he wasn't allowed through security. So he sent Danya on to board while he went to the front counter for his pass. The gentleman there told him he was sorry, but because Jason checked in less than an hour before the flight, he couldn't print Jason a pass.

Jason calmly explained. The man didn't care. Jason sanely explained again. The man still didn't care. Finally, Jason, now not so calm, convinced him to involve someone else in the process; so the man disappeared into a back room, and after what seemed like forever, finally emerged with Jason's pass. Nerve-racking.

With only minutes remaining before departure, Jason sprinted to the gate just in time to board. All seemed well. They arrived at the Detroit Metro Airport, grabbed their luggage, and headed for the bus that would take them to the parking lot where they would claim their car.

But a shooting had occurred in that parking area. Yes, a shooting, and now the lot was a crime scene under investigation, and no one was allowed in and no vehicles were allowed out. Unbelievable.

That's just how some days go . . . from bad to worse. Or was it?

I mean, they weren't stuck in Florida, far from their waiting children; Jason did receive his New York boarding pass; they weren't victims of the violent crime; and after several hours the parking area was reopened, and they did get their car. (Of course, after the lot had been closed for more than six hours, you can only imagine the crowds of people and the congestion of traffic trying to leave, but they inched their way through and made it safely home.)

In the early hours on the day of Jason and Danya's travel, at their home, Justin, their eight-year-old son, said to his other nana, "Let's pray that my mom and dad get home safely." Hmm, I have a feeling Jason and Danya's day could have been much worse without an intercessor.

God's mercies (compassions) are new every morning. I think we don't begin to "catch" His mercies because it's so easy, at least for me, to be focused on what's not working. This is a broken planet; we don't have to look far or long for troubles. They are crouching at our doorways, peering through our windows, camping on our lawns, and occasionally they move in with us. Just ask Walter Swift.

Walter was convicted of a serious crime in 1982 and sent to prison. This morning, this very morning that I'm writing, he woke up to his first sunrise out-side of prison in twenty-six years. You see, the courts decided he was wrongly convicted and set him free.

Imagine. Twenty-six years. When Walter was released yesterday, he was greeted by family and by a man who came to help him reintegrate into soci-ety. This man understood wrongful conviction because he was sentenced for rape and spent nine and a half years behind bars before a DNA test proved his innocence.

The man came bearing more than just a check to help Mr. Swift start his new life. He was a living extension of God's mercy. The road ahead will be uphill for Walter; he will need someone who under-stands his jagged journey. And unless we've worn prison issue, we can't understand the degradation. Unless we've had our daily choices stripped from us, we can't imagine the demoralization. Yes, this one who came to Mr. Swift with the dust of experience still on his shoes was a mercy gift.

Walter was asked on a newscast what he was looking forward to. "To talk to another person who looks at me and is kind." When asked what he plans to do next, he replied, "Take a walk." Then he said, "You'd think after being gone that long I'd want big things like cars and money, but it's the little things you miss most, like being treated with respect and being smiled at."

I pray for currents of mercy to carry Walter Swift above the dangerous undertow of bitterness in his mornings ahead. He has a colossal journey in front of him. May God guard his vulnerable heart. And may God remind us of His mercy toward us, which is bestowed anew every day, just as sure as the sun rises and shines its light on us.

Questions to Ask Yourself

❋ When was the last time your morning went askew?

❋ Who are the intercessors in your life?

❋ In what ways have you felt imprisoned?

❀ Who holds the keys to your freedom?

❀ List some new mercies in your life.

BRIGHT IDEAS

The apostle Paul spent a lot of ministry time in jail. Doesn't that seem like a detour of God's plan for him? Or a waste of Paul's zeal? Yet I can't tell you how many times when I'm feeling undone that I think of this verse: "Rejoice in the Lord always. I will say it again: Rejoice!" (Philippians 4:4 NIV). Paul was in prison when he wrote that.

Paul also penned, "In everything give thanks; for this is God's will for you in Christ Jesus" (1 Thessalonians 5:18). Everything? Cancelled flights? Jail time? Injustice? That's a big order, Paul. Or perhaps sometimes it's a process? Read Philippians 4 four times; I promise you'll be glad you did.

I think God's compassion enabled Paul to write while he was incarcerated, and I think God expresses

His mercy to us when we read what Paul wrote. The words written by someone in a hard place carry greater impact.

Don't tell me to cheer up if you've never known heartache or depression, but if you have paid the price of wisdom and soaked up God's compassion, please, oh please, come rain on me.

Tomorrow morning is a new day, fresh with God's mercies. May we purpose to catch a basketful of compassion and extend it to others.

❋

The path of the righteous is like the first gleam of dawn,
shining ever brighter till the full light of day.

—PROVERBS 4:18 NIV

four

Christmas Lights

*Blessed is the season which engages
the whole world in a conspiracy of love!*

—HAMILTON WRIGHT MABIE

I am a Christmas light junkie. I usually have seven trees encircled in lights and tucked, glowing, here and there throughout my home. They range from four to twelve feet in height. The latter is always a challenge for me to top with a luminous star. I've learned to scale a tall ladder, and with a clothes hanger for an extended reach and with much prayer, I flip the star or an angel onto the tippy-top.

(Don't attempt this tottering technique without a safety net.)

This year I've voted to give myself a reprieve and to have only one medium-sized tree for our grandchildren. I will decorate but with reserve. Now that's my plan. We'll see. I often start with a small plan and then go psycho. I end up decorating everything that doesn't move, which has caused concern for my husband in his recliner. By the time I'm done with my light shenanigans, I can't turn the power on lest I plunge our community into utter darkness. Well, actually the community's fine, but we can't vacuum without blowing fuses or flipping breakers or whatever it is that leaves us blindly feeling our way through the house. So too bad, vacuuming has to wait until January. Now that's a heartbreaker.

I confess I like the wonderland that lights create, especially when I see the eyes of my grandchildren. Last year Noah, who was then age four, came over. When he saw the twelve-foot, prelit, undecorated tree, his mouth fell open, and all he could say was, "I didn't know you had one this big!" (Evidently trees are like kids—when you don't see them for a year they seem so much bigger than you remembered.)

Well, the towering evergreen must have stayed on his mind, because the next morning he begged his mom to bring him back over. On the ride, Noah repeatedly told his mom, "I sure hope Nana will let me help decorate that tree."

When Noah dashed into my house, he made a beeline to the living room and announced, "Nana, I'm here to help you decorate that big tree."

"Oh, good. What a relief. I need a helper." I applauded. He glowed.

Noah conscientiously decorated the two limbs at his eye level. Nothing higher, nothing lower. It was precious. When he and his mom left, I thanked him for his significant contribution. "Great job, Noah." You could see pleasure fill him like helium.

A couple of days later, after I had finished the tree (actually, it had finished me), Noah came back over. I had the tree lit with a thousand tiny lights and hundreds of Christmas balls, bells, birds, and bows. When he stepped into the room, it took his breath away, and I heard him whisper, "Wow! I didn't know I did all that."

It usually takes days for me to put up and decorate that twelve-footer, and some years I've called in friends to help me finish it. And I'm not getting any younger. My husband's health doesn't allow him to help, but I don't think he misses being involved.

In fact, some of the tensest moments between us through the years have been over our Christmas trees. My usually jovial husband would lose his glee when it came to putting the live, unyielding tree into the stand. The children and I would drift into the nearest snow bank and take refuge there until he had completed the task of forcing the tree to stand erect in the holder. It was usually several feet shorter than it had started out, as Les attempted to straighten the trunk. But hey, who doesn't enjoy a Christmas bush?

Eventually we went artificial, which resolved Les's frustration. Almost.

But then that smoldering ember of exasperation rerouted into the lights. ("How do they get that tangled when I put them away so carefully?" he would sputter.) Between untangling them and lacing them through the limbs in a balanced manner, his huge heart would reduce to a pebble. No "ho, ho, ho" going on at that point, I assure you.

Ah, but then came the prelit artificial tree. And sure enough, Les's heart expanded twentyfold, back into the jovial Santa he truly is.

You know what? I'm not going to do it this year. Nope, no big tree. No gazillion lights. Just a sane, simple holiday with lots of love. Besides, we all need to help conserve our world's energy. We certainly are being made aware of that in these uncertain days.

I'm sure my family and friends will understand my not putting up the towering tree. Even the one who told me her Christmas highlight is to come for an evening around the tree. And the one who flies a far distance every year for a Christmas visit and insists on sitting . . . where else? Yep, in the room with the tree. In the cast of the tree lights, we giggle over cups of hot cocoa and voice future dreams. And I'm sure my neighbors won't miss the massive beam of Christmas proclamation through our front windows, which has sent out greetings to them for the past eight years. Surely the kids won't mind not sitting under the branches searching for their names on presents.

Oh, perhaps I could put up the tree, only with fewer decorations. And just light it at special times. I could leave the outdoor Christmas lights off the trees and bushes in our yard, which would help with conservation. And I could leave the snowman tree and the two wildlife trees in their boxes this year.

Actually, if I decorated the fireplace, the entry, and the kitchen area, that should be enough without the big tree. Besides, we go south after Christmas for four months; so why have all that hassle of packing up the tree dressing? And the endless trips down the steps to store it all. Why, I could use that energy in other ways. And then I wouldn't have to deglitter the house. Woo-hoo!

What are the holidays about anyway? Right. They're about Jesus our Savior. Although isn't He all about light? In the light of the angel Gabriel's presence, the heavenly messenger announced the coming birth to Mary. In the light of a dream, Joseph was divinely informed of Mary's holy conception. Starlight directed the wise men to the Christ Child, while the shepherds had their own brilliant night encounter with heavenly hosts who were praising God. And most importantly, the Light of the World, Jesus, filled the manger, the world, and now eternity.

Hmm, perhaps I will put that lit tree-tower up again: a luminous holiday reminder that we haven't been left without hope in this dark world.

Stay tuned.

QUESTIONS TO ASK YOURSELF

❀ What shenanigans get you into the most trouble?

❀ What overload causes you to flip a breaker switch?

❀ What task do you dread and put off until the new year?

✺ When did you last make a significant contribution to a task? To a person?

✺ What takes your breath away?

✺ What was the last argument you had with yourself? Who won?

✺ What are ways you can best use your energy?

BRIGHT IDEAS

My husband, Les, had never been fired before; so when he was "let go" at a new job, it took us several days to internalize that reality. Even though we found out his replacement was the owner's brother, who had just moved to town, we didn't find that information terribly comforting. What we knew was it was Christmas, and we were broke.

I'm not a visionary, so all I could think about was how we could buy a couple of presents for our kids. Twelve-year-old Marty was understanding, and three-year-old Jason wasn't aware of our plight. So it was more about my need to give to my children than their need to receive. Marty wanted a board game called *Life*, and Jason wanted some Matchbox cars. Both gifts were within our financial reach, but I was certain the boys needed more. Now what's that about?

It turned out, because of a friend who was dispensing of her son's toys he had outgrown (which included a basketful of Matchbox cars) and some generous friends who saw our need, we had a "rich" Christmas. As a family we used our creativity and ingenuity and put more emphasis on loving each other. Today that Christmas is one of our sweetest memories.

Who knew?

WAYS TO BRIGHTEN YOUR DAYS

Money matters, but being broke doesn't limit God's riches—practice gratitude.

Are you projecting your needs on others? Ask them what they need. Their list might be different from yours.

Don't get stuck on the "cover" of your life story; there's a bigger picture inside. Work on seeing the whole calendar, and not just today. Circumstances change . . . as do we. Whew.

Find ways to reflect God's light . . . become a tower. One day, when Christ shows us what we did for His kingdom, I pray we can be heard saying, "Wow, I didn't know I did all that."

❋

The message of Christmas is that the visible material world
is bound to the invisible spiritual world.

—UNKNOWN

five

Laser Light

I don't like that man. I must get to know him better.

—ABRAHAM LINCOLN

"Laser" forms the acronym for **Light Amplification by Stimulated Emission of Radiation.** Stick with me, girlfriends, and by the time this read is over, we'll be bursting with brains. Just think how handy knowing what "laser" stands for. Why, I'm almost certain you could add it into your breakfast chatter. Unless your morning is like ours, in which the first one to break the silence is in danger of being oatmealed. Then you might want to hold off until lunch.

Quite honestly, I'm not big on "light

37

amplification." And, no, it's not just because I'm older than King Tut's tutu . . . although there is that.

I've been known, when I'm light amplified, to frighten people with my lack of color. To say I'm fair-skinned is to underestimate bleach. I have to tent myself to sit outside on a sunny day. By the time I've slopped myself with sunblock, found my floppy-brimmed hat crushed in the closet, uncovered my prescription sunglasses in my purse debris, and then made my way over to my sun-filtered chair-spot under a tree—only to find that the pigeons from yonder roof have left "thinking of you" deposits—I'm quite over "light amplification."

Speaking of amplification . . . laser's narrow band of heat-directed light is quite the deal. Its value is expanding almost daily. Scientists have, in a sense, learned how to grab a handful of sunlight and funnel the power into precision uses. (I think some scientist just broke out in hives from my sim-plistic description. May I say, who better since you can whip up your own cure at the lab? In fact, try laser. I hear it's great on skin eruptions.)

Lasers are a multimillion-dollar business and were first demonstrated in a lab in 1960, which when compared to my birth date, makes it a baby. *Baby*, I say. And this baby has had an unbelievable growth spurt and is being used in CD players, DVDs, printers and ad pointers. It even reads the barcodes at the checkout line.

My husband used a laser level a couple of days ago when he hung a picture for me. (Thank you, honey. Sorry that I didn't like it there and that you had to rehang it in three other locations before it settled into its spot. I know you hate those nasty nail holes in the wall; so don't worry; I'm going to buy three more pictures to hang over them. Anything for you, Pookie-Bear.)

Laser can cut through steel and inscribe letters on computer keyboards. Laser is used in cosmetic surgery. Okay, now we're getting down to where the wrinkle grooves the skin. This is serious girl talk. We just moved from the practical to the necessary. Well, maybe not necessary, but often desirable. I would give this aspect of laser light an 8.5 on the

Richter scale as being a su

Christmas present. (Men, a word

sure she is asking for laser before you giv

spend the rest of your life trying to hang a ɳ

over that mistake.)

Unfortunately I'm not a laser candidate, since I'm allergic to the necessary numbing medications. Now your question is, "Patsy, would you really do that—have cosmetic surgery?" Do hormones fluctuate? Do underarms flap? Do chins double? Yes, honey, I'm an ardent supporter of "Any old barn can benefit from a new roof and a fresh coat of paint." (Although I did see a gal at the bakery the other day who obviously had a zealous "painter," because the skin on her jaw had been hiked up to her forehead, making her smile look like a grimace.)

Laser is used for many internal surgeries as well. The more frequent uses are to seal small blood vessels to lessen bleeding during surgery, to seal off lymph vessels to prevent cancer cells from spreading, and to remove tumors. Recently laser has been used on varicose veins and vocal-cord cancer. The

Japanese hope to develop magnesium-combusted engines that use seaweed and laser. (After all, the world's gas prices need surgery).

Probably the most well-known laser surgery is LASIK. The laser corrects refractive errors in our eyes. I, of course, don't qualify. Humph. What is it about my qualifications? But really, it doesn't matter because I love sending out search teams every hour to find my glasses, it's great fun looking at life through smears, I'd really miss the deep grooves in my nose, and I've become fond of the way bifocals magnify my eye bags. Nope, no problem here.

Speaking of attitude—we were, weren't we?—the Bible is its own form of laser. It's the Great Physician's favorite tool used, among other things, to excavate attitudes. And to talk about precision. Listen: "For the word of God is quick, and powerful, and sharper than any two-edged sword, piercing even to the dividing asunder of soul and spirit, and of the joints and marrow, and is a discerner of the thoughts and intents of the heart" (Hebrews 4:12 KJV).

Now, that's personal. When you start messing

with my marrow, I know I've been thoroughly examined. And then it really gets down to the nubbins when the exam includes a directed beam of light right on our thoughts and intents (motives).

Hmm, I'm not sure I want my motives highlighted. Why, even the possibility of my thoughts being known is jarring. I mean, sometimes the worst, nastiest, judgmental thought will skitter through my mind. Honestly, *I'm* offended by some of my thoughts—what must God think? Oh, that's right, He knows me. The Lord doesn't expose my stuff for His sake but for mine. That way I can take ownership and make changes. Sometimes all I can do to effect a change, considering my heart discrepancies, is to confess and relinquish. But often that's enough.

Yet other times I can do more to change. If, for instance, I have eye problems, which are expressed by judging other people's behavior, then studying, praying, and meditating on passages such as Matthew 7:1–5 would be a good laser procedure. I've found if I allow my eyes to stay focused on seeking truth, I'll see others differently. More mercifully.

I really don't want people to be harsh, dogmatic, or cruel in their evaluation of me yet Matthew 7:2 says, "For in the way you judge, you will be judged." That's pretty clear.

I've lived long enough—Stonehenge and me— that I've learned even when folks do spiteful things, they have a reason. Often when I know the reason, their actions make sense. It doesn't make them right, but it does make sense; and when I understand, I tend to be less critical and more compassionate.

Those who are regular grace givers tend to be those who have changed and grown because they have tenaciously sought truth with a whole heart. If all I have done is accumulate head information and not experienced heart reformation, I'm more likely to see others through tainted (similar to tinted, but darker) lenses.

While I was at Disney World with my family recently, we attended an indoor performance. My husband drives an electric cart not only because it keeps him mobile when he wouldn't be otherwise, but also to speed, yes, speed, lickety-split from one place to another. Because Les drove the cart indoors, he was ushered to the back row in the auditorium. We, his family, followed him (and if you haven't seen a family trotting behind a speeding handicapper, you haven't lived), and we were seated across the back. I sat between Speedy and my youngest grandson, Noah, while we waited for the performance to begin. Noah decided to make an announcement. In his outdoor voice he proclaimed while gesturing toward the audience, "These people are annoying me!"

I was startled by his volume, by his objection, and by his awareness of what the word *annoying* meant. I tried to shush him, which only inspired him to say louder, "Nana, they are annoying me," as he pointed to all the people in front of him.

"Honey," I protested in a strong whisper, "these people aren't doing anything to you."

The surrounding attendees peeked over their shoulders to catch a view of the antagonist.

"It's their heads, Nana. Their heads are annoying me."

I tried to assure him that, when the show began, everyone would be able to see.

Some weeks later, I exchanged e-mails with my daughter-in-law, Danya, and I mentioned how surprised I was that Noah knew what *annoy* meant and how to place it astutely in a sentence.

She responded, "I am so over 'annoy,' because earlier Noah announced that I annoy him." She was not impressed or amused.

I couldn't help it; I laughed aloud. It's so easy to be "over" people because, the truth is, we are annoying. I can annoy myself, can't you? No doubt my grandson needed a little laser on that attitude so he would have space for a tad of tolerance.

I feel your pain, Noah, only too well. It's back to Matthew 7 . . . again.

QUESTIONS TO ASK YOURSELF

❋ When was the last time God used His Word like a laser on your heart?

❋ What was the most recent incident in which you harbored an ungracious thought?

❋ What portion of Scripture helps you with your thought life? If you don't have a favorite, may I recommend Philippians 4?

❋ Who annoys you? (Be honest. God already knows.)

❋ What plan, with God's help, can you implement to overcome your sense of being annoyed?

BRIGHT IDEAS

When I think about attitudes, Old Testament Sarah and Hagar come to mind. Those two gals sure ended up annoying each other. Sarah gave her handmaiden Hagar to her husband to father a child (well, no wonder there was conflict). When Hagar became pregnant, more than her belly grew big. Hagar developed a highfalutin attitude. She decided she was better than childless Sarah.

Not bright, Hagar. May I just say it's never a good idea to snub your boss? No job security in that.

Sure enough, Sarah threw Hagar's pregnant self right out of camp. God met with Hagar in the desert, dealt with her, and sent her back—humbled—to Sarah's jurisdiction.

Years later, Hagar's son would cop an attitude with the son of Sarah (see, Sarah, you should have listened to God when He promised you a child). You know that didn't fly, so mother and son were thrown out, and this time they didn't come back.

Hagar probably hadn't heard that the apple doesn't fall far from the tree. Children often reflect the attitudes of their parents . . . and in some cases, ahem, the grandparents.

This week, meditate on Sarah and Hagar's story to see how God uses it in your life. (Genesis 16; 21:9–21.)

During Hagar's desert encounter, she called the Lord, "the God who sees me" (Genesis 16:13 NIV). How accurate that assessment is. Our God isn't in need of LASIK. He has perfect vision, and He is our light amplification. With a narrow band of light that He wields like a surgeon's scalpel, He can and does separate the soul from the spirit and the joints from the marrow, as well as discerning our thoughts and intentions.

I've learned to be grateful for God's deep inspection of my heart.

As we express our gratitude, we must never forget that the highest appreciation is not to utter words, but to live by them.

—JOHN F. KENNEDY

six

Flashlight

> *If children brighten up a home, it's probably*
> *because they never turn off the lights.*
>
> —UNKNOWN

If you live at my house, you will receive a flashlight for Christmas. It's a rule—unwritten—but you can count on it. Every year, whether you need one or not, a flashlight will be either in your stocking, in a gift box, or part of the decoration on top of a package. If it isn't presented to you by one of those methods, when you return to your bedroom, it will be blinking on your pillow, bedecked in ribbons.

Some years you might be lucky and only have to figure out what to do with a keychain version.

Other years, well, you may need a forklift to transport all of the gizmos to your room.

I can't pass up flashlight ensembles when I'm shopping. You've probably seen them. The packages include one for your shirt pocket and then the flashlights increase in size until you get to the flashlight of all flashlights. Designed to, uh, wave semis off highways, herd elephants, or serve as an emergency light for airport runways, you never know when you might need one of these enormous items.

A flash of light serves other purposes too. They are good to evict bogeymen out from under comforters and beds and out of closets. Not to mention how well flashlights work to make bunny figures hop on the wall. You can SOS buddies from across the street or find lost stuff. Good stuff. Like scruffy Life Savers, lint, dead bugs, Cheerios, chewed gum . . . .

My husband, Les, crams his myriad flashlights into drawers, glove compartments, and tool chests until they corrode over and have to be chiseled out. What's a man to do when flashlights fall into his life like manna? Occasionally he will put one under his

chin and then make a dreadful face to scare the bat-
tery life out of his naive wife. She does not laugh.
Trust me on this.

But the most fun I've experienced with a flashlight happened when I was a kid. I would go out with
my dad in search of—are you ready for this?—night
crawlers. More affectionately known at our house as
"bait." There's nothing like a big, fat, juicy worm for
threading on a fishhook and tossing in the lake.

You may not know this, but worm harvesting
takes a lot of finesse. You have to hold a flashlight in
one hand as you scan the terrain. Then, when you
spot the wet bodies gliding between blades of grass,
you drop, grab, and pull. Yep, pull. Some of those
worms are more than a foot long. No, I'm not from
Texas . . . well, part-time I am, but I'm talking about
true Michigan beauties. And there's a knack to pulling on them, or you will end up with a shorter,
messier version of the original.

Now keep this information in your bait bucket:
the best place to shine for worms is the golf course
right after the sprinklers shut off. Whoa, let me tell

you, those worms are healthy, slick, and fast. Even if you set your foot down too solidly, those shifty slitherers shimmy down into the earth quicker than you can work up a spit. And that's no fib. But if you can grab even an inch of worm before it wiggles its backside into the hole (this is where the pulling comes in) and then work his stretchy body out until its snaky form is dangling from between your fingers, you have a sweet victory to savor.

Now, for some of you, that's called oversharing. But I've told you the grimy details to ask you what would make a little scaredy-cat girl go out into the damp, dark night with her flashlight to search for and touch disgusting worms? Yep, to be with her daddy.

My dad had a small vocabulary when it came to his love language. He played crossword puzzles, took naps with the newspaper over his head like a tent, watched Kate Smith (you have to be old to know her), played poker (when my mom wasn't looking), and fished.

Mostly he napped. He was really good at it. It

may have been his gift. He could sit a deep chair and snore up a severe thunderstorm. He did sing "You Are My Sunshine" once in a blue moon. It's still one of my favorite songs.

So what's a girl to do? I wasn't mature enough for crosswords, I didn't like Kate Smith (sorry, but she came on at the same time as *The Nelsons*, and I had a crush on Ricky), and Dad wouldn't let me play poker (lest my mom scalp him, and he was already bald). So that left fishing. I seldom actually went fishing with him, but that was probably my fault. I guess fish aren't fond of whining, and I wasn't given to sitting still for hours. But to my credit I did know how to bait my own hook. Getting the whopping two-and-a-half-inch flailing fish off my hook— now that was a whole other topic.

My dad was a good dad. He worked all his life to pay our bills, and he loved my mom. But he just couldn't squeeze out enough emotional energy to give much to me, his needy daughter. I was high maintenance, and he was low energy, not a great match. Even though he did his best with what he had to offer, I grew up with a daddy-hole in my soul.

Maybe that's why I buy flashlights at Christmas. The worm-hunting expeditions are cherished memories, and maybe that's my way of holding on to them. Or maybe, with my little light, I'm still in search of my dad.

One night, as an adult, I dreamed that I was in a restaurant, and in the next booth I saw my dad. I got up stunned, heart racing, threw my arms around him, and wept for joy. But then I became aware he wasn't hugging back, and when I looked up, I could tell he didn't know who I was and appeared bewildered. So I asked him, "Don't you know who you are?" I figured he would say, "Sure, I'm your dad." Instead he looked at me, and with absolutely no emotion, he replied, "No, I don't."

And that was probably true. I don't think any of us fully grasp who we are, and few of us are able to fill our roles completely. I know, as I look back, I have a laundry list of things I wish I could change as a mom regarding my role with my sons. Today they are good men, but that result at times came about in spite of my efforts rather than because of them. I've had to work to learn to forgive myself for not being more mature and astute during my child-rearing days. Oh, all things considered I was a good mom, but my insecurities left a shaky imprint.

And I have forgiven my dad for not understanding the importance of his role as a father to a girl. How could he have known? His dad was the most unavailable, low-key person I've ever known. I have no memory of my grandfather actually speaking. Mostly he rocked, chewed tobacco, and spat in a rusty can. I read somewhere we get our role models from our same-sex parent and our sense of safety and security from our opposite-sex parent.

When I came to Christ, I wasn't aware that I would drag my dad-stuff into my relationship with God, but that's what happened. I'm told that we unconsciously respond to the Lord in the same patterns we responded to our earthly fathers. So if we had a nurturing, tender interaction with our dads, that establishes the same kind of bonding with our heavenly Father. On the other hand, if we had a dad who was unavailable, that relationship will impact our ability to trust and to feel safe in God's care.

If you're like me, you will always be trying to find ways to earn God's approval rather than resting in the truth that Christ permanently won God's favor on our behalf. I don't have to battery-up my flashlight to search for His love; I just have to open my heart and receive it. And while I know that to be a great truth, how does one do that?

Well, for me, it has taken flashes of light from God's Word to replace the old, dark messages and behavior. I keep a small tape recorder, and when I'm struggling, I'll read Scripture pertinent to my need onto the tape. The repetition of playing and replaying helps me to build a reservoir of truth. That then enables me to combat my old beliefs that I have to make points with God to be noticed—and that I have to do things correctly to receive approval.

I still struggle with bouts of shame when I don't live up to impossible standards I've placed on myself. But I'm grateful that I continue to make progress, as I give myself permission to make mistakes and even at times to disappoint others when I know I'm doing what I'm supposed to do.

I've noticed that, when I'm tired or going through a difficult season, I'm more vulnerable. If I'm not careful, I can slip back into webbed haunts. Also I realize a great source to keep me mentally on track is my friends. They know my susceptibility, and their insights act as flashlights of accountability.

Questions to Ask Yourself

❁ What about God is hard for you to believe?

❁ Why is that a struggle for you?

❁ What flashes of light from God's Word address these issues? (A concordance might help you to find these.)

❁ Who is in your circle of accountability?

❁ What type of "worm harvesting" did you do to win your dad's attention, affection, or approval?

❋ Have you forgiven him? (Depending on the degree of loss in this relationship, you may want to engage a therapist to help you through the maze.)

Bright Ideas

We can glimpse God's father-heart in Deuteronomy 32:4, 10–14. Sit awhile each day for a week and consider the attributes recorded there. Write them down. Review them. Believe them.

Here are a few I've found, to help you start.

In verse 4, we see God's strength, stability, and permanence. We're reminded that God's works, His actions, are perfect. And that He is fair in all His dealings. (We don't have to gather worms to win His heart.)

In verses 32:10–14, we see that, as our Father, He finds us even in our howling waste places. What a descriptive term, "the howling waste of the wilderness." The word *waste* comes from the Hebrew root meaning "desolation, desert, confusion, emptiness, and vanity." (This means that, even if I'm whiny and can't sit still, He searches me out.)

Scripture goes on to say that Father God encircles us, cares for us, and guards us. What a protective picture. Allow that kind of care to saturate your thoughts. Pause and meditate on it.

There's so much more in those verses, but I wanted to jump-start your thinking about God's kindness toward us as a Father. I'll let you take it from there.

If you find it hard to carve out time to study and meditate, may I make a suggestion? Slip a flashlight under your pillow, and then, before you doze off, click that baby on and read a few verses.

Don't have a flashlight? Hey, let me know; I'll put you on my Christmas list. Sweet dreams.

❀

As old as she was, she still missed her daddy.

—GLORIA NAYLOR

seven

Purse Light

> One disadvantage of being a hog is that
> at any moment some blundering fool may try
> to make a silk purse out of your wife's ear.
>
> —J. B. MORTON

Anita Renfroe is a spunky gift-giver. She gives laughter and thoughtfulness as generously as bees give honey. Recently she bestowed on a number of her friends, me included, purse lights.

What are they, you ask? They are ingenious tiny light-up boxes that clip into the lining of a purse, and they come in kicky patterns. With one push of the button, this light allows us to find lost articles, even if they are hiding in the dark folds at the bottom of our bags. And we girls know that our purses hold the potential to be the Bermuda Triangle.

I know that some of you keep your purses as tidy as your desktops, and I would reward you, but I dropped your trophy in my bag, and it hasn't been seen since. I'm one of those who endlessly stir around in the rubble of my belongings, fingering the mysterious debris in search of buried treasure, and whose desk resembles a ripe compost site.

Okay, maybe I'm not that bad, but I am a frustrated purse-r. I needed Anita's light. That's one of the great things about light-bearing friends, especially when they step into our lives to help light-en our load.

My purse contents are troubling. I carry too much. I keep trying to edit my belongings, but by the end of a day, my purse is once again pulsating. Yesterday I pulled a traveling coffee container out of my purse, and I don't even drink coffee. Don't ask. But every night it's something—or many things— that have hitched a ride in my bag.

I've tried smaller purses and have caused many a

petite pouch to exceed its stitches and spring a leak, or in my case, a creek. Too bad I don't carry paddles. When petite didn't help, I switched to monstrous bags, thinking then I could at least contain my stuff. Ha! I could hardly lift it I had the purse so full of what-ifs and maybes.

This isn't a new struggle in my life. It's a perpetual issue, and it spills over onto my desk, into my closet, and into my drawers. If we clipped the purse lights inside of those places, the gig would be up. I mean, I present a tidy appearance. At first glance, my home is clean and neat, and even my car is shipshape. Yet step in closer, and my stuff starts to seep up from the crevices. I definitely have a throwaway problem in that I don't wanna.

I think it might have something to do with Les and me being poor for a long time. Of course, being poor can seem to add hours to any day; so maybe, in the grand scheme of things, it wasn't all that long ... but long enough. I mean, we had a rental, but our furnishings were other people's discards. We were clothed, but we wore things others had tired of, and we always had food, but only because of the supplementary help of others. That's a very humbling position to be in.

Employee theft resulted in our losing a business, and we had to pay off debtors; so there was no jingle in my purse for several years. Every penny went toward what felt like an endless resolution.

Even now, years later, before I throw an item away, I still tend to think, *What if I might need this?* So really, what we're looking at is a response pattern born out of past experience that needs to be dipped in a vat of fresh faith.

Do you have any messy situations in your life for which you need fresh faith? When the Israelites were in the desert, they were given manna from heaven every morning, but they were instructed to not collect up more than a day's worth. Yet some did. I don't know if they slipped it in their purses for safekeeping, but wherever they stashed it, the manna turned to worms. Ew. Now that's messy (see Exodus 16:4; 19–20).

Was that a test of obedience? Or trust? Or a

visual of hoarding? Hmm, maybe all three.

On a human level, I understand why they thought it would be smart to fill their pantry, don't you? I mean, if you had struggled with hunger, and Pizza Hut delivered more than you could consume, wouldn't you put the rest in the freezer for next week? Is God puzzling, or am I the only one who doesn't get what He is up to much of the time?

We can miss God's higher call when we're busy trying to figure Him out, challenging His decisions, and being self-protective. We can't reason with God. Try as we might, He is above reason. Reason is about us. Sovereignty is about Him.

Yes, God's ways can be baffling, and may I say, we have our own peculiar behavior. Haven't you observed someone's actions and exclaimed, "What was he thinking?"

Take, for instance, the parable in which Jesus spoke of the servant who owed his master a debt and begged to be given time to pay it off (Matthew 18:23–35). The master was moved by his servant's pleading and forgave his debt. That same servant then went to collect money owed to him by a man who was unable to pay, and that man pled for mercy but didn't receive it.

This parable is about forgiveness, but as is the way with God's Word, it's full of additional take-aways. What struck me is how tightly the servant clutched his purse, his purse stuffed full of his rights. He had been shown mercy, but toward another he was merciless. How could he not extend the same grace he had just been given?

What arrogance. What insensitivity. What selfishness.

And yet ...

I've done that very thing. At times I've implored God to forgive me and then consciously tucked a grudge against someone else into the recesses of my bag, occasionally flashing a purse light on it to make sure it's intact. What was I thinking?

Before going to bed each night, I find if I dump out my purse to sort through the contents, it helps keep down the debris. I sort, throw away, store, and then carefully place things back in my bag. Sounds like it might be a good idea to do the same with my heart. Except I'm not very objective when it comes to my own heart debris. That's where I have to depend on the Holy Spirit to help me throw out what is unnecessary, store what is good, and carry with me what is expedient.

Questions to Ask Yourself

❀ What's in your purse? Any secrets?

❀ In what area of your life would you win a trophy for tidy?

❀ Who helps to light-en your load?

❀ Define fresh faith. Do you have it?

❀ Have you ever been poor? For how long?

❀ Are you a hoarder? Why?

❀ Does your purse's content portray your heart's condition?

BRIGHT IDEAS

Probably the most famous purse of all is the one filled with thirty pieces of silver that Judas received for betraying Christ (Matthew 26:14–16). What was Judas thinking? Was he so driven by greed that the silver was all it took to tip his scale? Could he be bought so easily?

Judas had been with Jesus. He had witnessed miracles. He had broken bread with the Savior. Yet Judas gave Jesus into the hands of the enemy for such a paltry sum.

What a reminder of our capacity to sin. We think we would do it differently, but truth is we're all capable of dastardly deeds. So how do we guard against committing spiritual betrayal?

The Bible tells us to "love the Lord your God with all your heart, and with all your soul, and with all your mind, and with all your strength" (Mark 12:30). So obviously it will take focus, dedication, and vigilance if we're to be full-hearted in our walk. Jesus paid the once-and-for-all price for our salvation, and now He invites us to be active participants in our growing-up. Learning sacrificial love is the most protective move one can make against betrayal ... of any kind.

HEART-PROTECTIVE
LOVE ACTIVITIES

Sit quietly for a while every day and listen for God's voice.

Get up and do three things you know you should do.

Ask forgiveness of someone who needs to hear it from you.

Extend mercy to a hurting person.

List what you are grateful for.

Tuck these love reminders inside your purse. Clutch truth to your heart. It will help you to be assured you've got it in the bag (groan). No, really, all purse words aside, allow God to click on a light inside the lining of your heart ... you won't regret it.

❋

As the purse is emptied, the heart is filled.

—Victor Hugo

eight

Lamplight

Light is good from whatever lamp it shines.

—UNKNOWN

Do you know of a good lamp-ologist? I'm in dire need. I have a bad case of lamp-itis, a condition that causes you to break out in lamps until they outnumber your brain cells. Right now I have more lamps than Jelly Belly has jelly beans. Well, almost.

Last week I had thirteen lamps lined up on my living room floor waiting for a nook to light up. My hubby and I sold our Texas winter nest and brought the accumulated belongings back to our home in Michigan, which, by the way, already was bulging with lamps. I was thinking maybe I should call that motel that leaves the light on for you and tell them, "Have I got a deal for you!"

My lamp collecting started years ago after a visit with my Memphis friend Nancy. Nancy is the kind of gal you wish you were (speaking for myself). Nancy is thin, attractive, clever, and artistically gifted. She's the right height and weight and is astute.

Do you think that's fair? (Another question I have when I settle into heaven.)

When I met Nancy, I immediately was drawn to her friendly Southern manner. Her hospitality followed suit. Every time I was near her home, she had me as her guest, which I loved. Nancy's house, like the owner, was full of charm. It's the type of place one dreams of but seldom owns. Actually, Nancy had added a great deal of the character and warmth to the abode. Style was just her way.

On one particular trip during which I had the joy of being Nancy's guest, the first night at bedtime, I watched her move throughout her home turning off lamps. I hadn't realized, until she switched them off, how many there were, and how much charisma they added.

When I mentioned the lamps, she told me where she had found them. Most were from yard sales or antique shops, or were castaways that she had rewired and restored.

I was fascinated. Then I became motivated. And now I am addicted.

Lamps litter my premises. Much to my husband's dismay. Les prefers ceiling lights, floodlights, torches, and bonfires. The more glaring the light, the happier he is; while I, on the other hand, like to huddle near a lamp in search of enough rays to read my large-print Bible.

I think lamplight is homey, warm, and romantic. My husband finds it restrictive, aggravating, and unnecessary. Hmm, perhaps we need a lampologist and a relationship-ologist? Nah, after forty-six years, we've learned to give each other space . . . so he goes to a room with enough light to flood a sports stadium, while I tuck myself in next to the dim beams of a glowing urn. Oh, sure, we take turns visiting each other, me bedecked in sunglasses, and him carrying a blazing torch.

Okay, so it's not quite that bad, but honestly, our internal electrical wiring was installed by two different electricians.

May I just say that the older I grow, the fonder I become of soft lighting. I really don't need any high-wattage enhancer to display my flaws. Eek!

When I was young, I used a splash of foundation and lipstick, but now I have a front loader for my "products." In the past, I used a sponge for application; now I use a trowel for the mortar and a weed whacker for the, uh, weeds. So for me, lighted morning mirrors are more jolting than a double espresso.

I'm not sure why Les isn't as smitten with my lamps as I am, because I've been selective. Yes, I have all sizes, shapes, and colors, but they are hand-picked. I have rabbit-shaped lamps (you have to keep tabs on them; they have a way of multiplying); I have urn-shaped lamps, oriental lamps, a light-up rooster who oversees my kitchen, ones that are dripping in prisms, pairs that stand together, floor lamps, ginger-jar-shaped ones, a teapot lamp, and even a light-up turtle. Of course, that doesn't count my lantern collection or my oil lamps, and please don't get me started on flashlights (you've already read about those in a previous chapter anyway). I'm working toward going green, so I'm sensitive to energy use. Therefore I take turns clicking on my lamps. Seldom, if ever, are they all brightening up the place at the same time.

Remember the TV series I Dream of Jeannie, and how she popped out of a lamp every week and granted wishes? I don't have one of those. Looked for one. Wanted one. The closest I got was a garage sale lamp from which a sculpted winged creature climbed out of the bottom and scared about three years of wattage out of me.

Speaking of wattage, did you know that the longest-burning lightbulb has been burning for one hundred years? No, I didn't make that up. It hangs at fire station #6 on East Avenue, in Livermore, California. During all those years it has only been turned off a couple of times; the rest of the time it's been doing what it was created for. The bulb, dubbed "The Centennial Light," is now listed in the *Guinness Book of World Records*.

If I had to select a lamp out of my collection to give an award to, it would be the one that was custom designed just for me. Little ol' me. And guess who made it . . . my husband, the old lamp disser himself. By happenstance my hubby found he had a knack with stained glass, but he also faced a challenge. You see, Les is colorblind. But he overcame this hurdle by enlisting a friend and me to pick the colored glass for his projects and label them. He took it from there. One of his lamp creations has more than four hundred hand-cut pieces.

I was impressed as I watched Les huddle over a pattern with all those glass fragments, which he patiently placed. When the pieces were strewn around the workbench, it looked like chaos; yet once they were soldered, the lit brokenness turned to beauty. That lamp carries an enlightening message about the beauty God can make out of brokenness.

I love when a lamp is lit inside of me that has never been turned on before . . . usually. Oh, sure, sometimes a defect is illuminated that's hard to consider. But that's called owning our stuff. Sometimes the Lord will do this lamp lighting through His Word, a person, the arts, nature, or circumstances.

Recently I was explaining—okay, griping—to a friend about an interaction I had with someone that didn't go well. When I finished, my friend told me I was wrong. How rude was that?

But that day she was like a lamp with a three-way lightbulb because she kept turning up the brightness of light beams on a flaw in my character that had held me in relational angst. Yet I hadn't seen it, as I sat in the dark with the flaw as my companion.

When my friend and I finished our conversation, I knew she was right. Now I'm asking God to transform my brokenness . . . to direct a heat lamp toward that flaw so that, not only will I become healthier, but also so the Lord might shine more brightly through me. And I'm searching God's Word for light-giving counsel on "character." And, I must say, there's a lot there.

Girls, I'm not shooting for the *Guinness Book of World Records*, but I would like to be a Centennial Light that keeps doing what I was created for . . . shine.

QUESTIONS TO ASK YOURSELF

❇ What items, emotions, or circumstances litter your life, like my profusion of lamps litter mine?

❇ Who has influenced your choices, like Nancy affected my love of lamps?

❇ Are you doing what God created you to do?

❇ What is in fragments in your life?

❇ Has someone shone a revealing light on one of your flaws? How can you shine God's healing light on it?

Bright Ideas

Because of my passion for lamps, it only follows suit that I also love lamp verses from Scripture. I find them warming as well as enlightening. Pools of light are like that—they beckon us to draw near and curl up in comfort or cast aside hesitation to step forward.

"Thy word is a lamp unto my feet, and a light unto my path" (Psalm 119:105 KJV). In this verse, the word "lamp" means "prosperity and instruction." So we can say the Word is what adds wealth to our existence, is what we hold dear, and is what adds value to our lives. It serves as a light-bearing compass that leads us to wise counsel and direction.

In my personal journey, more often than not God has guided me to the pages of a book to find counsel. Usually that book is the Bible, yet many times He has used the writings of others to point the way for me. As much as I appreciate Bible aids, such as commentaries, I find the Scripture to be its own commentary, for when we diligently search

God's Word, it defines and affirms itself. The light of truth glows brighter and brighter.

I use commentaries to find out what others are thinking, and often they enhance my understanding by bringing to light customs from Bible days and meanings of Greek and Hebrew words that Scripture was originally written in to showcase a word's dimension. In translating the Bible from its original languages, translators often had to settle for a single meaning when the initial word had a much wider breadth.

My formal education is limited; I'm neither a theologian nor a scholar, but I am a zealous student. My dim understanding has been and is being "lit" by the lamp of God's Word. I'm grateful that we are promised the Holy Spirit will "guide [us] into all the truth" (John 16:13). I rely on that.

Don't allow your education, your lack thereof, or your age to keep you from being teachable. For me, teachable means we have space inside of us to willingly hear. Once we've heard, we measure the merit of the information next to the counsel of

God's Word, and if it's consistent, we willingly embrace it.

This week, turn on your brain lamp and investigate a verse or chapter. Read the surrounding verses to gain the context. Pray for enlightenment. Write out the verse. If your Bible has a center column of connected verses, read those as well. Check a commentary to see what insights someone else has on the passage. Ask three people who are spiritually savvy what they think the verse says. Meditate on the verse. Then ask the question: how does this fit inside of me? You're bound to find the experience, uh . . . enlightening.

❋

*I am never long . . . without yearning
for the company of my lamp and my library.*

—LORD BYRON

nine

Candlelight

A candle loses nothing by lighting another candle.

—JAMES KELLER

Do not, I caution, do not light your perfumed candles in my vicinity. I am combustible. Okay, okay, maybe not combustible, but I am scent reactive—big time. Oh, how I wish I could bask not only in the glow of candles but also breathe in the yummy fragrances available to us today. 'Tis not the case. When I'm in a store, my body can tell if I'm within twenty feet of a candle counter. My temples thump like the drums of Tahiti, my sinuses run like the bulls of Barcelona, and I wheeze like the beached whales of Malibu.

83

And even though I love travel, that's not the way I want to experience it.

I have loved candlelight since Jack jumped over the candlestick. In fact, when I was a child, prior to fragrance infusion, I even had a candle business. My friend and I rolled store-bought tapers in glue, then glitter, and went door-to-door selling them for one dollar per pair. My favorites were light blue candles with bright red glitter. I was a gaudy kid in search of a career. Candles would not be it.

Speaking of careers, I read an article about a candle company that helps battered women. They say that the slow candle-making process has proven to be a healing procedure for the women's war-weary emotions. The company was donated to the shelter in hopes it would provide skills and some finances for the women. They've named the company Light of Hope—how appropriate.

But candles don't just help to light up a woman's world. Ask Mr. Husbands. He was diagnosed with cancer and needed something to do to help keep his mind off his treatments. So a friend took him to the store to buy a candle-making kit. That flicker of interest has turned into a flame of passion that shows up in his kitchen, where every container in every cupboard is full of wax.

Husbands discovered that area churches were discarding used candles, and he lined up for the leftover wax. That supply allowed him to make enough candles to sell. A friend stood on the side of the road to peddle them for Husbands, and with that money Husbands bought more supplies.

At the time of his diagnosis, Husbands was told he would probably not live long. Now, a decade later, he's hoping to open his own candle company.

Maybe that's what I need to do, open my own fragrance-free candle company. Perhaps I do have a career in candles after all . . . Nah, I think I would need more than three customers to stay in business. I'm aware that most of the world is clamoring for the smelly stuff. In fact, now companies are layering the smells like trifles . . . Eucalyptus Kiwi Lavender Watermelon Delight. Oh, my aching head.

While I can't get up close and personal with

perfumed offerings, I do applaud candles' graceful appearance, and their ability to glow hope.

When I sat in the dark world of agoraphobia, I was surprised by hope when it first appeared as glints: it would flicker in the phrase of a book; it would light up the line of a song; it would radiate through a verse in the Scriptures; it would glow in a phone call from a friend; it would warm me during the prayers of my husband; it would glimmer when someone expressed an unexpected kindness; it would illuminate the smile of my child. Never underestimate small offerings . . . Think of them as candles, and while we may not be able to light the world or fix someone else's life, we can offer hope, which on its own creates quite a blaze.

A Chinese saying suggests, "It is better to light a candle than to curse the darkness." That truth is worth pausing over and caught my attention because I'm given to highlighting the negative before I discover the positive. I'm not sure why that is—temperament, perfectionist tendencies, or just human proclivity—but I continue to work on that discouraging flaw. I gain inspiration from others.

The folks of Pine County, Delaware, inspire me because instead of cursing the darkness they are literally lighting candles. At the Relay For Life for cancer survivors, they place luminaria (candles in paper bags), along the high school track in memory of those who have died fighting cancer. Those who are still in the throes of the battle and those who have won walk to raise money for research.

Instead of being depressed over their losses, they are celebrating their loved ones' lives. Instead of forgetting the problem, those left behind are helping to find a cure for others, as the contributions for these candles are used to help battle the dread disease. (I love the word *instead*; it reminds us we have a choice.)

I'm especially moved by those diagnosed with cancer. My dad, mom, and aunt all died from cancer. My sister, cousin, and best friend are battling it now. I have lots of reasons to light candles and to applaud their relay for life.

And I'm well aware of my high risk, but then

life is risky, isn't it? We have the safety of knowing we are Christ's, but we aren't privy to what a day will bring. I'm grateful we're promised that Christ will give us strength to bear our pain.

The weather was lovely outside, but a thunderstorm raged on the inside the day my great-nephew Joshua was diagnosed with leukemia. Because of a six-hundred-mile path between our front doors, I hadn't met Joshua until he was four years old and was airlifted in dire condition to a hospital near our home. His parents, Mike and Michelle, moved in with us, as they fought for their young son's life.

I remember vividly those scary days, when Mike had to lie across his son's little body so the doctors could perform painful procedures on him. And the distressing memories of when Michelle had to carefully clean out Joshua's port while he howled his protests. Just as clearly, I recall his constant demands for food, an appetite that was created, fueled, and magnified by his medication. We took shifts fixing eggs for him to help keep his panic at bay.

Joshua made many trips back and forth between

his home, our house, and the hospital. But Josh made it! This week he graduates from high school. And every year he walks in the Relay For Life with other cancer survivors in his area. He continues with great vigor to carry candles high in gratitude, in remembrance, and for the cure.

Michelle and Mike had no idea how strong they were until they journeyed through the valley of the shadow of death. I don't think any of us knows what we are capable of bearing or doing. And I don't think anything is more frightening than knowing your child is in jeopardy. It plunges you into devastating vulnerability and desperation.

For many years, when I heard other people's bad news, I moaned, "I could never bear that." Since those years, I've gone through some crushing blows, much more than I thought I could bear, only to find that in my weakness I discovered new levels of Christ's strength. The candelabra-truth that our God rises up mighty in our weakness blazes throughout Scripture, as God's people repeatedly fell on their faces in fear and rose up in courage . . .

Moses, when confronted by God's voice in a burning bush, was told he would lead his people out of captivity. What a moment. Think of it, to be designated by God for such a task. What a referral! And what was Moses' response? He suggested God send someone else instead because Moses didn't speak well. He sure underestimated God, didn't he? But the story goes on and so does Moses, for he may have knelt down stammering, but he rose up a robust leader who blazed paths to the promised land.

Moses is just one of throngs in the Bible who were tempted to be more certain of their weakness then they were of God's strength.

Add my name to that list. What about you?

Questions to Ask Yourself

❀ Are you emotionally war-weary? What has brought you to this place?

❀ What would cause you to glow with hope?

❊ What small kindnesses might you extend to others to shed some light in their lives?

❊ Are you naturally more positive or negative? Would others agree with that answer?

❊ How could you be a blazing candle for "your people"?

❊ Do you underestimate God? How?

BRIGHT IDEAS

I think my friend Carol Edwards must have hung out with Moses. No, I'm not suggesting she's old, but she has risen up out of a childhood weakness to impressive adult strength. See what you think . . .

From the age of seventeen months until she was six years old, Carol's address was a TB ward in a sanitarium. That's more than four years . . . four formative years. When admitted to the sanitarium, Carol wasn't even two years old, but emotionally she knew that "her people" were no longer available to her. How confusing. How scary. How lonely.

When she did go home at the age of six, her parents had divorced, her new stepfather was a hard man, and her world looked big, unfamiliar, and scary. (The only time she was allowed to go outside during her hospital years was onto the rooftop for a breath of fresh air.)

If I understand popular beliefs, Carol shouldn't be a healthy, balanced person capable of contributing to society. What she endured in the way of abandonment, isolation, and restrictions could have been permanently disabling, leaving her fearful, relationally stunted, and bitter.

Yet today Carol is a candle lighter of the finest kind. She's funny, kind, engaging, bright, energetic, and a delight to be around. She volunteers for Stephen's Minister, a nondenominational outreach of those who come alongside the hurting. She is a compassionate listener who understands her weakness and God's strength.

In God's economy, our weakness is nothing,

nothing, (one more time) nothing in the presence of His strength. He can guide us through paths of recovery, restore lost years, and give us a firm foundation.

Make a list of times when you have knelt down weak and risen up strong. Rehearse them until you have them securely fixed in your heart to reference the next time you find it hard to be courageous or the next time you get to share your flame to light someone else's candle.

※

There is not enough darkness in all the world to put out the light of even one small candle.

— ROBERT ALDEN

ten

Headlights

*I was like a deer in the headlights. There are
just some days when you and your partner
aren't clicking. For some reason, we had to
fight through every element in a negative way.*

—GARRETT LUCASH

Les and I have caught more than one deer in our
headlights, but then how could we help it—we live
in Michigan. Last year an estimated nine hundred
thousand deer resided in our state. Heavens to
Bambi, that's a lot of venison!

I didn't grow up eating venison because my folks
were originally from the South, and they were big
into fried chicken, pork chops, and meatloaf. I was

fifteen when I joined my friend's family for a week's summer jaunt to the Upper Peninsula of Michigan, where venison was a staple. Venison often was featured in a Finnish meat pie called a "pasty." No, not a Patsy, but a pasty. Layers of venison, diced potatoes, onions, rutabaga, and carrots are wrapped in a lard-based crust and baked. Yum.

The pasties were wonderful, but I couldn't quite get used to venison. I think I saw Rudolph too many times to be objective. But I was introduced to one other new item that summer that suited my taste perfectly—my future husband, Les. Now, honey, there was a dear in headlights. Well, actually I saw the headlights on his Oldsmobile Rocket 88 before I caught a glimpse of him, as he jetted past me.

By the time I left the tiny hamlet tucked into the shores of Lake Superior, I was in fifteen-year-old, heart-twittering love.

Les and I have been married for forty-six years, and I still delight in seeing headlights coming toward me, when he is at the wheel. (Be still my heart.)

Growing up, Les lived in a woodsy location, very different from my suburban upbringing, and his lifestyle fascinated me. He worked as a lumberjack and a commercial fisherman; he hunted, fished, mined copper, and trapped mink, beaver, and weasels. He was so macho. Oh yes, and he was an altar boy at a Catholic church, and to prove it he could say prayers in Latin.

When I was growing up, I lived in a bustling township outside of Detroit where, as a young girl, I took tap and ballet lessons and walked to the local library. While Les was working in the woods, I was watching cartoons, reading Archie comic books, and complaining I had to make my bed once in a blue moon. I was so prissy. And oh yes, I was a Baptist, and to prove it I could recite all the names of the books of the Bible from memory. *Touché*.

When the Upper Peninsula married the Lower Peninsula, we both looked like deer caught in headlights. We were totally unprepared for each other's . . . uh, unique offerings. It's easy when we do things

differently to judge the other one instead of applaud-
ing. Too bad it can sometimes take us so long to
appreciate each other's contributions. But eventually Les and I realized that without the other one
we would each have a huge hole in our hearts.

Today, after forty-six years of marriage, we still
spat, but mostly over inconsequential things. Things
you would miss even with bright headlights. I'm
grateful we don't hold on to our spattage (like "wattage," just not bright). I think many of our nitpicky
tendencies are based on the need we each have to
control.

Recently, my man bought us red motor scooters
(without warning). Motor scooters! Here's *my* warning: rush your children into the house, pull your
drapes, and go to the center of your homes because
. . . Patsy's got wheels!

Les must be delusional to believe his meno-
pausal woman should be set loose in a neighborhood
with one of these jazzy little roadrunners. He was
sweet to convey such confidence in my ability to
handle this adorable scooter. And honey, it scoots!

Ask me how I know. Go ahead. No, really, I don't mind. I mean, I already embarrassed myself in broad daylight in front of God and any amused neighbors who were peering out their windows, so why not announce it in print?

Honestly, anything that requires more than three steps is outside my mental sphere.

(1) Turn key to On, (2) squeeze brake, (3) push button (uh-oh), (4) turn handle slowly (too much info), (5) brake on both sides.

"Don't hang your feet out the sides; this is not a bicycle," my sons called to me repeatedly as I exited our steep driveway (with my feet out the sides).

I wobbled like a Weeble down the road. I drove ever so slowly, trying to get the hang of this bright red vehicle and then came to a halt at the stop sign. Whew!

That's when things went wrong. Very, very wrong. I must have hit the gas. I would blame Les, but I was the only one on the bike. Suddenly it took off for Nebraska. I jerked the handlebar hard to the left and managed to stay on the road, but in doing so I must have hit the gas again, because the roadster bit into the pavement and then bucked. Yes, bucked like a bronco! I was all over the street, feet flailing out on both sides, trying to wrestle it under control. Ha! Somewhere in my rodeo stunt ride I must have released my death grip on the gas, because it slowed and came to a stop. Well, the bike stopped, but I was a ball of quiver.

My son Jason drove up at that moment. He had witnessed my wild escapade as he came down the street. "Why didn't you just let go of the gas?" he asked. My answer is not worth the price of ink.

Jason shook his head and said he had never seen anyone come that close to the cement and not wipe out or die.

I took it as a compliment. It was, wasn't it?

Really, some people should just knit.

Okay, okay, I'll try again tomorrow . . . maybe . . . when no one is looking.

Anything in your life out of control? Maybe it's time to let go.

QUESTIONS TO ASK YOURSELF

❄ Who was your fifteen-year-old love?

❄ Who is your dear in headlights now?

❄ Do you celebrate differences between yourself and others?

❄ Where has spattage built up in your life?

❄ How have you wiped out lately?

❄ What area of your life do you have trouble giving up control in? Why?

BRIGHT IDEAS

When I start up my scooter, the headlamps immediately light up, day or night. I like that the lights are never an issue because they are always on. That's the kind of faith I would like to have—when I awake in the morning or in the middle of the night, I'm good to go.

Jonah was that kind of prophet. He awoke, received orders from headquarters, and scooted away. Oh, no, wait, he tore off in the wrong direction. I hate when that happens—when I know what to do, and I deliberately choose not to 'cause I don't wanna. That's out-and-out rebellion, willfulness, taking control. Not a pretty picture. And, of course, Jonah's story is proof that when we think we know best and we hold onto our ways, determined to hang onto the controls of our lives, we can go pretty low.

Remember when the sailors were trying to find out the culprit who had caused a god to bring such treacherous storms against them? The lot fell on Jonah, indicating to the sailors his guilt. I can imagine at that moment Jonah felt like a deer in headlights. Caught, Jonah suggested the sailors throw him overboard, so they did. Yikes! Watch what thou asketh for.

In the windowless belly of a fish, Jonah reconsidered his runaway choice. Isn't that interesting? In the darkest locale, he saw clearly. Hmm. What's that about? I wonder if we underestimate hardship's potential to light the way. Or the potential of a solitary space for reflection. Or that a failure can lead to firm resolution. (Won't do that again.)

Oh, here's a side note for moms: we might want to think before we rescue our children too quickly from suffering the consequences of their bad behavior. It could be the motivation they need to change direction.

I recently received an e-mail from a woman who told me that her mother turned her in to the police because she was using heroin. She was nineteen years old at the time, and she was sent to prison. In a tiny cell while going through withdrawal, she invited Christ to redeem her life. She cried out, "I can't survive this alone! Change me." He did. She said, "I felt peace and light come over me. It was as if someone turned on all the lights in the prison and inside of me."

When she relinquished control of her life to Christ, He changed her and her future. Soon after her conversion, she was moved to an alternative prison for nonviolent crimes where, while serving out her time, she was named the most improved inmate.

That was a heart-wrenching, brave choice her mother made. The daughter recognizes that her mom saved her life . . . and Christ saved her soul.

Turning in a new direction isn't easy, but Jonah and this former addict are proof that, with God, it can be done.

So if you're driving your scooter toward disaster . . . let go . . . let God.

❀

Whoever loves his brother lives in the light,
and there is nothing in him to make him stumble.

—1 JOHN 2:10 NIV

eleven

Reading Light

The road to knowledge begins with the turn of a page.

—UNKNOWN

They march down mantels, spill onto tabletops, crowd baskets, peek out from cabinets, huddle in countertop corners, beckon from bedsides, nest near the fireplace, stack in corners, and conspire, shoulder-to-shoulder, on shelves throughout my home. I'm speaking of the books that fill my life with information, beauty, pleasure, and joy.

Have I read them all? Well, no, but like many things, I plan to. Someday. I'm a habitual reader; so I've turned many a page, and I encourage others not to miss the life-expanding adventure of a good book.

I often have to go through the volumes filling my home and cull. That's not easy for a committed book lover. I give them to friends, church libraries, and occasionally a stack finds its way into my daughter-in-law's garage sales.

I love bookstores, especially privately owned ones with rickety floors and reading corners touting paunchy chairs and good lights. Light is imperative at this juncture of my reading career. Yep, I'm a career woman. I'm committed to reading all the days of my life and encouraging others to join in the life-fulfilling fun.

I enjoy books on CD as well, but for me they could never replace the tactile experience of holding a book and perusing its pages. Yet the audiobooks offer me company on trips, in hotels, during waits at airports, or when I'm too tired or too sick to pick up a book.

Since I'm in the long season of menopause, may I say to any sister comrades who might be hot-flashing their way through this book, that one of the common changes for us is our sleep patterns. What a news flash, huh? But if that's true for you and you find yourself with "extra hours" on your hands, I recommend you listen to Scripture and praise tapes on headphones. I keep mine next to my bed, and instead of clicking on the reading light, I click on my CD player. I see this as a way to redeem those awake hours, and often I'm lulled back to sleep. It sure beats mental fretting and churning.

I actually didn't become a full-fledged, dyed-in-the-wool reader until my mid-twenties. Reading began as an act of desperation for me, to help pull me from the dark pit of agoraphobia, but later it became my education, inspiration, and passion. For years I couldn't afford to own books, so I borrowed from all my friends' libraries. Then they ran out, so I opened a bookstore in a back room of my house. I took books on consignment, reading them gingerly, so as not to muss the pages, and then sold them. I was book-hooked . . . book, line, and, uh, inker.

This caused me to be drawn to other readers because I found them to be well-developed thinkers and able to articulate their thoughts with verve. That was inspiring. Also they were downright interesting because they had well-seasoned minds.

I find it fascinating how often a book has been the impetus for life change. Take Chuck Colson, the founder of Prison Fellowship, who while serving a prison sentence for his involvement in Watergate, was given a copy of *Mere Christianity* written by C. S. Lewis. That was the beginning of a new life for Colson, who since his release has used his energies to help prisoners (and their families) survive the severity of prison life. And it all began because of the influence of ink, words, and paper.

The word *obituary* grabs a person's attention because death is really never far from our minds. Imagine, though, if you opened the obituary column and discovered you were the subject matter. Now that could ruin your Saturday.

That's what happened to Alfred Nobel, the inventor of dynamite and many other explosive items and weaponry. Hearing you have died is enough to tie-dye one's shorts, but to read your obituary and find you have been portrayed as a villain, well, that's a whole other kind of nasty jolt.

The obituary writer penned Nobel as the "Merchant of Death." I would call that a lit stick of explosive material dropped on a guy's creative ego. The columnist probably waited until Alfred's supposed death before he pinned him with that name lest late one night his roof mysteriously blew off into the Milky Way.

Well, those words depicting his achievements in such a defamatory manner caused Mr. Nobel to reconsider his legacy, and he set out to change that sentiment. He took large sums of his wealth and established the Nobel Peace Prize, honoring those who made major contributions to bring about world peace. Many other fields of endeavor were recognized including medicine, economics, and, hooray, literature.

Nobel's family probably wasn't thrilled that Alfred, at his passing, left a major part of his financial estate to the coffers of the Nobel Prize. But just think—Nobel's new life passion began because of what he had read.

Thomas Jefferson believed the nation's leaders needed expanded reading resources; so in 1814 he seeded the small library by selling to the government his personal collection of 6,487 volumes, more than doubling the Library of Congress's offerings. Today that has swelled to one hundred million items to form the world's largest library.

Author Hazel Rochman expressed her love of reading by saying, "Reading makes immigrants of us all. It takes us away from home, but, most important, it finds homes for us everywhere."

My home is all about books. Occasionally someone will ask me the title of my favorite book, and I have a list, but always at the top is the Bible. Now, that sounds like a pat answer, but trust me, it's not. No other book I own or have ever held means as much to me.

I have one-hundred-year-old Bibles, brand-spankin' new ones, hardcover, leather, and paperback. I even have a Bible from the family of R. E. Olds, the founder of the Oldsmobile car (retrieved out of discards from the Salvation Army forty years ago). I have my grandmother's threadbare Bible, my mother's well-traversed one, and the small white one I carried down the aisle when I married my husband forty-six years ago.

Today some of my ongoing favorites are my study Bibles. For those I need a comfy chair, a table, pen, paper, a magnifying glass (yes, I'm owning it), and of course, a really good reading light beaming over my shoulder.

One of the many things I love about reading my Bible is that every page, every verse, every word is backlit, illuminated by God's Spirit. And while an overhead reading light helps us not to ruin our eyes, the Holy Spirit opens our eyes so we don't ruin our lives. The words pulsate with life. And those words are not conjecture, opinions, or gossip, but the unadulterated divine truth. Truth that changed my heart, my mind, my direction, my marriage, and my profession. (Prior to being a speaker, I was a professional phobic . . . and, honey, I was good at it.)

I encourage folks to begin reading their Bibles

with this prayer: "Open my eyes that I may behold wonderful things from Your law" (Psalm 119:18). For me, that prayer is like flipping a switch that reminds me to allow God's Spirit to usher me into truth and not to fling myself into the murky depths of speculation. Left on my own, honestly, I could come up with some pretty strange doctrine. I need the protection of the holiness of the Spirit's guidance. He is my Reading Light.

Between the covers of the Bible is a library—sixty-six action-packed, change-your-life books. So where does a person start? Hmm, the opportunities are endless. If you're new to the Scriptures, I recommend the gospel of John and the book of Philippians. If you're more familiar with the Bible, you might enjoy revisiting Genesis (nothing like a fresh beginning). And if you're a scholar, please, come sit by me. I'm thirsty for your well of wisdom.

I'm a Proverbs fan. I love the down-to-earth, in-your-face, practical truths it holds. But I would caution you that Proverbs pulls no punches and leaves us little wiggle room to squirm out of the convictions those verses can lay on us. These pro-verbial gems can be like battering rams that crash into the hard places in our hearts. It's eye-opening to discover how much the human heart is self-seeking and cordoned off.

But the verses can sometimes generate tender "aha!" moments in which insight fills us with warmth and understanding. God has used Proverbs both to gain my attention and to win a greater share of my affection.

For a moment, let's turn on our reading lamps, lean in, and consider this consoling thought: "When you lie down, you will not be afraid; when you lie down, your sleep will be sweet" (Proverbs 3:24).

This kind of comforting rest is preceded earlier in that chapter with the instruction to "keep . . . wisdom" (v. 21), and then later in the chapter, rest is promised to those who do (Proverbs 3:21). Here's the question we need to ask: "Do I keep wisdom?"

I can only speak for myself. I'm a keeper of things. I keep teapots in cupboards, I keep books on mantels, and I keep lamps on shelves. Do I keep wisdom?

Well, sometimes I visit wisdom like I might a person I respect, but do I keep her? I've had her in for tea, and we've had warm conversations, but she didn't stay.

I recognize wisdom because she's a soft kind of strong, and I find that winsome. She's not rude, but she's clear. She's not pushy, but she's bold. She's only off-putting to those who are opposed to her clear ring of truth.

But do I keep wisdom? I like her a lot, and sometimes she spends the weekend, but keep her? Mmm, not in the way I know I should.

See, I told you, Proverbs corners you and bids you to grow up. It focuses the reading light on what we need to see.

But I hedge under the interrogation of its words. I know I want to lie down and not be afraid, I want my sleep to be sweet . . . but according to this flash of truth, I must first invite wisdom to live full-time with me. I must be willing to keep her close and respond to her counsel even when she requires me to change.

Truth be known, those times when I'm afraid, like a child, I just want God to make the scary thing go away. These light-bearing verses help me to understand the grown-up truth that living wisely is the precursor to peaceful nights of rest.

Years ago I wrote a ditty I wanted to have tattooed on my nightshirt: "Our Shepherd Never Slumbers So Sleep, Sheep."

When I'm actively making an effort to live wisely, I find that then I can lie down in quietness that leads to rest. And to ensure sweeter rest before I drift off, I read a few Bible verses, allowing them to nest in my mind. Then I turn off my reading light, and . . . ahh, sleep. Do I always then sleep? Uh, no. But when my mind is full of God's Word, I don't brood or work myself into a mood or mental frenzy.

Today the weather is gloomy. Hooray! Rainy days used to make me melancholy, but now they give me a reason to flick on lamps, and those hospitable pools of light invite me to cuddle into a chair and read. I keep small stacks of books within easy reach for such a time as this. Reading can feel like such a luxury when so many things are tugging at our time, and I've found if I put off reading until it's convenient, it won't happen. So I try to squeeze it into real life.

I have an idea. Why don't I retrieve one of those stacks and tell you what my reading light will soon illuminate? Just a minute. Okay . . . here goes: *Time Peace* by Ellen Vaughn (my second time through this one); *A Good Yarn* by Debbie Macomber; *Collected Stories* by Willa Cather; *Intimacy with the Almighty* by Chuck Swindoll; *David* by Beth Moore; *From Battle Scars to Beauty Marks* by Ellie Lofaro (second time); and *Experiencing God Day by Day* by Henry Blackaby and Richard Blackaby. Whew. That's an ambitious stack and will fill gloomy days with light . . . the light of their wisdom.

Sometimes I'm focused on a single book, but other times I'm flipping pages on two or three simultaneously. That can be dangerous, because in no time at all I have Willa knitting with Debbie's yarn. Or I'm quoting Beth when it was really Chuck's lines.

If I'm not careful, I can do the same thing with

Bible study because I tend to read hither and yon—a dab of Genesis, a dollop of Matthew, and a dose of Paul. I find a better way to dip into the Bible is to stick with a book or a character until I'm thoroughly acquainted, instructed, and inspired before I dash off.

I heard about a gentleman who read through the Bible four times a year for thirty-five years. Now that's impressive. I would have loved to have known him. The Scriptures must have been imprinted across his heart, and I bet they oozed out of his every pore. I'm sure it layered him in wisdom.

The wonderful thing about Scripture is that you can't exhaust divine truth. It's dimensional. A verse can unfold one way at a certain point in your life, and then unfold another way at a different time. That's part of the illuminating mystery of God's words and His ways.

If I could bless you with something, it would be a flame to read. Reading can be the key to opening up the universe or, at the least, opening up our minds so our hearts can grow.

Questions to Ask Yourself

✸ How many books do you own?

✸ Which books are especially precious to you? Why?

✸ Do you have favorite books in the Bible? If so, what are they? If not, perhaps this would be a good time to search one out.

✸ When is the last time a Bible verse had your name all over it?

✸ Have you ever read through the Bible? If not, will you consider doing it this year? It's a worthy goal.

Bright Ideas

One of my sweetest childhood memories was my grandmother's dedication to her daily Bible reading. She would pull a wooden chair up next to the window, open up her large-print Bible, tilt it to catch the sunlight, and with her bifocals low on her nose and her handheld magnifying glass positioned over the Scriptures, she would read.

As a child, I watched with interest; as an adult, I remember it with pure admiration. Oh, did I mention she had a third-grade education? Or that she continued her reading discipline until she fell and broke her hip when she was ninety-six? She never recovered from that break, and without access to the window, she had to rely on others to read to her. Mamaw was a ninety-seven-year-old wonder . . . and then she went to be with the One who had filled her window and her heart with sunlight.

I have one of Mamaw's Bibles, which I will pass down to my grandchildren. And I'm building a children's library to hand down as well. I so delight in children's stories and playful illustrations. I take pleasure in a well-told tale that dances across a child's mind and fills his thoughts with colorful adventures. I want the future generation of children in my family to applaud books, to love reading, and to have hungry hearts for knowledge.

When my oldest grandson, Justin, was six, I gave him a set of Dick and Jane books. I was excited. He had a different take on ol' Nana's gift choice. When he pulled the wrapping paper off the package, he looked at me, heaved his shoulders, rolled his eyes, and scolded, "Nana, you always give books. Books, books, books!" Then he finished with a scowl, "I have enough." (Justin and his mom immediately left the room to have a gratitude chat.)

A year later, Dick and Jane books were among Justin's favorites to read. Yes! Don't give up encouraging those around you to be readers. It may not "take" on the first dip into the word pool, but eventually you'll hear them splashing around with joy.

❊

If kids are entertained by two letters,
imagine the fun they'll have with twenty-six.
Open your child's imagination. Open a book.

—UNKNOWN

I realize not all books are created equal; we must be selective. Mark Twain said, "Be careful of reading health books. You could die of a misprint." And while Twain was jesting, some books can make us head or heart sick, but don't throw the light out with the discards.

Just as I'm preparing a legacy of books for my grandchildren, you've received a legacy that has enriched your life in some way. What has been handed down to you? What legacies are you leaving? What can you prepare now that gives your heart joy to think about your family inheriting?

❋

*I know every book of mine by its smell,
and I have but to put my nose between
the pages to be reminded of all sorts of things.*

—GEORGE ROBERT GISSING

twelve

Starlight

There they stand, the innumerable stars, shining
in order like a living hymn, written in light.

—N. P. WILLIS

We've celebrated stars in countless poems, songs, and movies. If that's not enough, wise men have followed them, foolish men have worshiped them, science has spent billions studying them, sweethearts claim them, artists paint them, sculptors chisel them, gazers track them, jewelers mount them, and children make wishes on them (along with some adults).

We're told by science that stars are massive, luminous balls of plasma. Oh, right. So they say. That explanation doesn't begin to capture the magic, the beauty, the mystery, and the romance of these light-bearing night diamonds that dangle from the heavens by silver threads. Never seen the threads, you say? You're kidding. Ask a child. She will help you discover them and so much more.

When my youngest was, uh, young, I spent untold hours hanging the heavens in his room. Let me just say it looks easier than it is. Who knew? No wonder God took a break on the seventh day.

I know you've seen those stick-on, luminous stars sold in a package. Well, that's what I used to establish my son's universe. Probably not the same quality as starting from scratch, but I wasn't sure how to whip up a ball of plasma; so store-bought had to do. Turns out that press-on stars, once pressed, mean business. You know the kind of stickum where, when your child is bored with the constellations and you have to remove them, they take wallboard and sheet rock right down to the studs with them? Yeah, those.

I still remember standing on Jason's bed and stretching (and I have marks to prove it) to position the bulk of the twinklers straight over his pillow.

When my heavenly creation was done, his buddies took turns lying on the floor with the lights off, oohing and aahing at the hundreds, yes, hundreds of stars that covered the ceiling and sparkled down the walls. (Actually, God was far more lavish. I read that one hundred billion stars are in the Milky Way alone. Hello.)

Stars capture the attention, appreciation, and applause of all ages. They are like the night's fireworks. And we all love those clear nights when we can immediately spot Alkaid, Alcor, Mizar, Alioth, Megrez, Phecda, Merak, and Dubhe—a.k.a. the Big Dipper. They are part of the constellation of Ursa Major, the Big Bear. I know this because I just copied it out of a research book, lest you think I'm a star junkie or a Chewbacca wannabe or something.

I also read this: "The Earth's axis is tilted relative to the perpendiculars to the ecliptic plane by an angle of 23.4° (separating the celestial and ecliptic poles by the same angle), which causes the circle of the ecliptic to be tilted relative to the celestial equator again by the same angle, which as a result is called the *obliquity of the ecliptic.*" That was when I realized I was in way over my head. If you understand this paragraph, may I suggest that you need to get out more? Besides, anytime we talk "tilted axis," I get dizzy.

Back to the stars. The aforementioned star names (Alkaid, Alcor, etc.) are man's designated tags for them. They already had God-given names, but since folks didn't know them, they gave the twinklers new names, and I personally don't think the stars are impressed.

You know what they say, once a Patsy always a Patsy. When I was young, I dreamed of being called something else. I mean, I was no starlet, but who wants to be a Patsy? Yet, when I was old enough to change it, I didn't. Names go deep inside us and add to our definition.

God tells us He named the stars (Psalm 47:4), and I just know He was more creative than "Phecda," know what I mean? (Psalm 147:4). I tried to imagine what God might have named them, but my best guesses were Dazzling, Stunning, Vivacious, and

Sparkling. I know those are kind of lame when you think of heavenly creations. I bet the stars have names we've never heard of, and when they finally are spoken aloud, our hearts will dance in joyous celebration. That's just how God does things.

After all, aren't you smitten on a clear, star-studded night with not only the sky's brilliance but also the deep sense of God's sovereign plan? God's creative genius always is beyond us. I think that's so we're reminded there really is Someone out there who has an amazing plan set in place.

In Scripture I've noticed that some of His "stars" went through name changes: Abram became Abraham, Sarai became Sarah, and Saul became Paul, to name three. Notice how the root stayed the same in each new name but the word was divinely tweaked.

Abram not only had a name change, but he also received startling news. God had him look up at the stars, and then God announced to the ancient man that he would have as many children as the stars. Well, hello, Abram was a hundred years old and had no children. But here's what I think made Abram stunning—a real Phecda. We read that, when God told him about his future family, Abram believed God. Abraham believed God could accomplish the humanly impossible. And it happened! Abraham became the father of the Jewish nation. Shine, Abraham, shine (Genesis 15:5–6; 17:5).

Out of all the folks in the Bible, no one has more names or shines more intensely than our Bright Morning Star, Jesus. He is called Savior, Redeemer, Shepherd, Counselor, King, Living Water, the Way, the Door . . . and the list goes on. He is all we need and more. I have to say, one of the names that I love the most is Christ the Light of the World (John 12:46). Our light.

Perhaps that's because I lived my teen years in spiritual darkness and then my young adult years in depression. Rebellion keeps you from caring about stars, and depression keeps you from even seeing them. But Christ came and sat with me on my starless nights, waiting for me to realize He was there. And when I did, it changed everything.

I had thought God was mad at me for all my mistakes. Instead, I learned that Christ had died to take on our sin, and when He did, He took on God's wrath. Christ paid the price so that God would never again be angry with His children. That kind of revelation, when internalized, opens up everything for us—from our heads, to our hearts, to the star-filled heavens. Suddenly the darkest night becomes, as N. P. Willis says, a backdrop for "a living hymn, written in light."

QUESTIONS TO ASK YOURSELF

❋ What does your name mean?

❋ Does that define who you are becoming?

❋ Do you think of God as lavish? Why?

❋ Which of Jesus' names is your favorite? Why?

❋ Have you ever believed God for the humanly impossible? What happened?

✻ Was there a time you thought God was mad at you? When did that feeling change?

Bright Ideas

When was the last time you heard Jiminy Cricket croon, "When You Wish Upon a Star"? No kidding, that long? Don't deny yourself one more minute. Go to YouTube (yes, right now) and type in the song title. Then get ready to be showered in sweet memories. You'll thank me later.

When I was reading about stars, not only did I visit Jiminy, but I also went to Wikipedia, where I read this statement: "Astronomers can determine the mass, age, chemical composition, and many other properties of a star by observing its spectrum, luminosity, and motion through space."

Even though I'm committed not to delve into my "mass" or "age" (thank you very much), I was drawn to the words "spectrum," "luminosity," and "motion." Here's what I thought. All three of them have to do with light and energy, and I wondered, *When I'm observed, what do others see?* Am I passionate about my responsibilities? Do I look beyond my discomforts and applaud what I'm privileged to have? Do I enter my days with purposed vigor? Do I search Scripture with expectancy? Does my behavior protect the dignity of others?

I think approaching life in these ways helps us to develop a wider spectrum, an enhanced luminosity, and motion that is deliberate and matters. Because I think we all ponder deep down the questions, "Am I star material? Am I shining brightly enough? Does my contribution matter?"

If you were to join me on the lawn some clear night, we could look up into the sky and study the visible stars, each sparkling with a different intensity and each one adding to the divine fireworks. Their separate contributions and constancy give us dimension, hope, and light. What a visual!

Shine, girlfriend, shine!

❈

Let your light so shine before men, that they
may see your good works, and glorify
your Father which is in heaven.

—MATTHEW 5:16 KJV

thirteen

Exit Light

*As you exit the plane, please make sure to gather
all of your belongings. Anything left behind
will be distributed evenly among the flight
attendants. Please do not leave children or spouses.*

—UNKNOWN

I always feel better when I spot well-lit exits. Maybe because I'm often in large crowds of people, and it just makes good sense. Or perhaps I'm slightly claustrophobic. Then again, it could be because my sixty-inch height puts me in jeopardy of getting squashed like an ant if there's a mass exit from a room. Whatever the reason, whether I'm in a hotel, on an airplane, or in an arena, I'm comforted when

I have a clear way of escape. Of course, what looks like a way out may not be . . .

Twenty years ago, I was at a women's conference and had just finished doing book reviews onstage. I thought the singers were following me off the platform and out a side exit that emptied into a back hallway. But I didn't realize the couple had detoured to the right and had sat down in the audience. So, when I stepped into the soundproof hall and the heavy exit door clicked shut behind me, I was all alone . . . almost.

A man reached out and grabbed my arm. Startled, I tried to pull loose from his grasp, but he had a secure grip. He demanded that I take him to a celebrity speaker who was scheduled to participate in the program. I told him I couldn't do that because she hadn't arrived yet. He became agitated and murmured something about people like me. His tone alerted me the statement wasn't a compliment.

By this time I realized that this man was potentially dangerous (duh) and that I was half a football field away from where we might encounter people, with lots of dark side rooms between safety and me. I knew I could never open the door behind me before he twisted my arm off, and at that juncture of my life, I had grown quite fond of my parts. Forsooth, that was the arm that held my hand that brushed my teeth, and I needed it.

To make matters worse, the man rattled on about how he had just been released from a facility for the criminally insane. Now that was comforting. He told me that, when he was arrested, the police had found him dressed like a woman in a women's restroom. Oh, great. He was going to break my arm and take my new Ann Taylor shoes. Right then I made up my mind that I couldn't afford to be a victim and decided to take charge, all five feet of me. To say I have an intimidating presence would be to suggest Minnie Mouse could threaten Darth Vader.

Scripture tells us that "God . . . will provide the way of escape" (1 Corinthians 10:13). My eyes did a quick survey, but I saw no obvious exit. Then an exit idea came to me, and I tried a different approach, since wrenching my arm back hadn't worked. "Come on," I said with authority. "I think our guest has arrived, and I'll take you to her." (Now, that is what one would call a big, fat lie, but at that moment it looked like a lit exit sign to me!)

Vader loosened his grip, I pulled my arm free, and I took hold of his arm and led him. That felt better—as if I had some control. Control is such a slippery eel. The entire way, I gabbed like a magpie on caffeine about how much I had always liked this guest he was obsessing on. As we neared the lobby, he saw people milling around and grabbed my arm like a vice clamp. After what seemed like the longest walk of my life, we entered the lobby and a friend's husband spotted my stressed countenance and commented to his buddy, "I think Patsy might have a problem."

Well, yes! Hello!

The two men came over, and while one started up a friendly chat with Darth Vader, the other man stepped in between him and me, which encouraged the man to release my arm. I was then quickly ushered into a side room full of staff. My legs turned to Play-Doh, my heart ricocheted, and I teared up. A half hour later, Les arrived, and I fell into his arms and bawled like a baby. So much for Mighty Minnie.

From that encounter I learned that, if one exit sign doesn't work, look for another way out.

Although, I have to add, at times I've exited when I should have stayed put. School was one of those times. Throughout my high school years, my brain was muddled by a dark sadness and a purposed rebellion. I became very self-absorbed and was certain I knew what was best for me, so I headed for the nearest exit and quit school.

The unaddressed emotional struggles of my teenage years grew into full-blown depression and agoraphobia throughout my twenties. I thought I would never find the way out of the suffocating panic that seemed stuck on spin cycle. But with God's counsel, I did. Not easily. Not quickly. And not without help. Some exits are long, windowless corridors. Don't give up.

Once I exited my emotional tsunami years, I found myself with a hangover of regrets. "If only I had finished school" was an incessant message that stomped all over my self-esteem and kicked me square in my confidence. Until finally I went back to school, took some classes, and then passed my GED. By this time, I was forty years old and speaking all over the country. That's when I learned that, as sweet as it was to have finished something I had started decades before, the diploma didn't heal the hole in my soul.

Don't misunderstand. Going back to school was a great choice, even a balm; but it was not the absolute cure for feeling good about myself. It was like trying to fill a well with a ladleful of water. It was the right idea, but not enough on its own. I think I held the belief that the more I accomplished, the more complete I would feel inside.

My friend Miriam Conrad was an accomplisher. She was strong, determined, and capable, but underneath her achievements was a raging river of pain, rejection, and anger. She felt far from complete. You see, Miriam's pastor-father sexually abused her, starting at the age of five. Her mother, who suffered with manic depression, never wanted Miriam. She begged her husband to give Miriam away, but her father couldn't figure out how to explain the missing child to his congregation. So they kept Miriam, but her mother never called her by name. Ever. If she had to speak to Miriam, she called her "you."

Miriam grew up to become a wife, mom, speaker, and author. And she became one more thing . . . a closet gambler. When Miriam's pain couldn't find an exit, it burbled up as a consuming addiction. That's when those who loved her and could see her undoing created an escape for her with an intervention, which led to a long, windowless corridor of counseling and eventually out a lit exit. Recovery makes the corridor worth the trek. Press on.

That Miriam survived as long and as well as she did was a succession of miracles, but she was on borrowed time. We can't hold down our unresolved issues without suffering from addictive behavior, health issues, relationship blocks, depression, fears, bursts of inappropriate anger, or unexplained bouts of sadness.

I can't begin to understand Miriam's nightmare

of pain, the confusion it had to cause her about God, and the wrenching abandonment issues with her mom. But I sure can see how it could lead to a pleasure-producing addiction, a secret way to cheer herself up and to distract from the persistent ache. Of course, as with all addictions, the pleasure is temporary as the vice splinters our dignity, sets us up for duplicity, and leads to self-disgust.

Miriam bravely faced her history . . . again. Yes, again. You see, earlier in her adult life she had received some help to sort through her upbringing and to deal with her adult obsessions. She thought she was done and all that was behind her. But, as is often the case, we face as much as we can bear at the time, and when our pain eases up, we jump back into a busy life, which can be another addiction.

Miriam's background was a convoluted corridor full of dark side rooms that she needed to turn the lights on in. With help and time, she is making her way to the exit, and while her history goes with her, the intense pain of her story no longer whirlpools below the surface, controlling her choices.

I personally have found pain will leave a residue, but God uses that to keep us tender and compassionate toward the fractures in other people's lives.

Questions to Ask Yourself

✺ Is there something in your life you need to find an exit from?

✺ Who could help you?

✺ When will you do it?

✺ What are your addictions?

✺ Do you have residue pain from your history? How has that helped you to help others?

Bright Ideas

We see God's people exiting en masse in the Old Testament. *Exodus* in Greek is comprised of two words meaning "out" and "road." The Israelites, who had been prisoners of the Egyptian pharaoh, traveled a road out of slavery. I believe it pleases God's heart to give us an out . . . really, isn't that what Jesus is all about?

In the book of Exodus, we see God providing for His people a way of escape and then making provision of water, manna, counsel, victory, and boundaries. I encourage you to read and review the first twenty chapters of Exodus. That will take you from their captivity through to the Ten Commandments. If reading all those chapters sounds like too hefty a read, then study chapters 15 through 20. That will take you from the song of Moses to the Ten Commandments.

Speaking of song . . . If you are given to whining, a song is a great way to exit that unproductive habit. It's difficult to be a full-on whiner while you are singing songs of gratitude.

As you read, you'll note the Israelites seemed to have an addiction to whining, which smacks of immaturity and anger. They paid repeatedly for their childish behavior. I can so identify. Having been a whiny child and a whiny adult, I recognize now the high price it exacted from my personage and my reputation. And unless I'm purposely working at being a "big girl," I can still slip down that slide. When I was a kid, we used to sit on pieces of wax paper to help us zip down a slide. Trust me, whining propels one down into self-made gloomy troubles.

I encourage you to tape these bright ideas on your morning mirror:

Look for the exit!
Never give up!
Press on ... and sing, sing, sing!

✺

I will love the light for it shows me the way.

—Og Mandino

fourteen

Streetlight

Hello lamp-post, whatcha' knowin'?

—PAUL SIMON

Streetlights smack of childhood espionage and grown-up brilliance. As a kid, when the streetlights flashed on at dusk in my neighborhood, we knew we had better boogie home. I was usually close by my house playing tag, hide-and-seek, kick the can, or baseball with my friends; so when the lights blinked on, I didn't have far to go.

Sometimes my friends were streetlight buddies out of necessity and sometimes out of convenience. For instance, the boys would never have allowed girls in the baseball games if they had other nearby choices.

I remember one time I walked around the block, and some kids were in an empty lot playing baseball. Just then the ball came rolling toward me, and I scooped it up and threw it back to the pitcher. It was the best throw of my life. The boys hooted and yelled for me to come and join them. From that point forward I did nothing right in the game. I must have used up all the baseball-ness in me with that high-flying throw. I struck out every time I was up to bat, I missed every high fly that came to my position in outfield, and I threw like a . . . a girl. I could tell the boys on my team were relieved when the streetlights came on, declaring an end to the agony. We all dispersed, and I slid into the safety of home base and the plate (heaped with food), which my mom had on the table waiting for me.

Streetlights weren't just about curfews, though; they were also about mystery and romance. Remember the classic movie *Singin' in the Rain* with Gene Kelly? I love the scene where he nimbly swings around a lamppost with the flame of love at his dancing feet. In the rain, no less. There should have been a public announcement with that scene, "Do not try this at home," because Gene was lithe and made it look so easy. It wasn't. Unfortunately, I found I wasn't any better at streetlight dancing than I was at baseball.

And who can't conjure up a mental picture from TV and movies of a private eye leaning against a lamppost, fedora pulled snugly down to his brows, the brim curled to shadow his downcast eyes, as he fiddles with a frayed newspaper? Occasional furtive glances up and down the fog-encased street would stir the imagination. Oh, the intrigue that brews in the shadows of a streetlight.

Of course beyond curfews, mystery, and intrigue, streetlamps do provide needed light. Oh, yeah, there is that. When my husband was growing up, he lived in a small town in the Upper Peninsula of Michigan. How small was it? They had eight streetlights. In the whole town. I had that many on my city block.

I remember the first time I arrived in his

hometown, it was nightfall, and believe me, it had fallen. It was the darkest dark I had ever been in. The heavy cloak of night made the house we were to stay in look creepy, so creepy that my friend Carol and I didn't want to get out of the car. We were teenagers, and don't tell, but we cried when her mom made us step into the thick blackness and wade through it into the "haunted" house.

All that drama could have been eradicated with a streetlight or two, because when morning came, we found the house wasn't scary at all. Unusual, but not frightening. Although we did find out later it was common for bears to stroll around town at will. Hello. Bears? Call me silly, but if wild varmints are going to mosey at will, I say to the city council, "Flip a switch, honey! Jam a few more poles in the ground and light up the place." But hey, that's just silly me.

Streetlights originally were designed and installed to illuminate street signs to assist travelers and pedestrians in finding their way. In 1880, Wabash, Indiana, took the title of being the second electrically lit city in the world. In the world! Now that's impressive.

Since then, many styles of raised street lighting have been installed globally, all with the intention of bringing light into dark places, although some have a more creative bent than others. Hershey, Pennsylvania, which dubs itself the sweetest place on earth, lines its streets with Hershey's Kisses-shaped streetlights, and the air is filled with the smell of chocolate. Talk about intoxicating! Pagoda-shaped light diffusers top lights in portions of New York City's Chinatown. And the streetlights in Roswell, New Mexico, are designed to look like a white alien's head with black, odd-shaped eyes painted on them. Ooh, spooky.

A year and a half ago at the Women of Faith conferences, Nicole C. Mullen was invited to be a guest performer, and this beacon of light arrived with a busload of streetlights in tow, in the form of her team. Nicole's team consists of mostly fourteen-year-old boys and girls who sing, dance, and quote Scripture. Talk about brightening up an environment—these kids are high-wattage. Collectively they rock the house with their youthful vigor and talent. Individually they inspire with their open hearts, eager to learn and love. They are polite, funny, smart, and lively.

Recently I asked the kids to share with me a Bible verse that I could pray for them. It was touching to read the verses they chose and why they selected them. Nicole's steady investment and the faithful guidance of their families are paying off in mature dividends. These dedicated young people work hard to study, practice, and perform. If these kids are a sample of what we can expect of the next generation, get ready, because they are about to light up the "road signs" of faith globally.

Shine, children, shine!

QUESTIONS TO ASK YOURSELF

❋ Who were your streetlight buddies when you were a child?

✻ What was your childhood safe place? Home? Your grandparents' house?

✻ When was the last time you danced in the rain?

✻ Where and when was your darkest night?

✻ Ever stayed in a spooky house?

✻ Are you eager to learn? To love?

✻ Who are you making a steady investment in?

✻ What have been the dividends?

Bright Ideas

Road signs worthy of streetlights:

Slow

"Everyone must be quick to hear, *slow* to speak and *slow* to anger" (James 1:19; italics mine).

I'd hate to have someone tally the number of times I've sped past this road sign because I wasn't slow to speak or slow to anger. Thinking I understood before I actually did, I've popped my cork, and then later when I slowed down enough to hear, I owed a passel of apologies.

Jumping to conclusions may be the only exercise some of us get, but it will never tone our faith, just expose our frivolous tendencies. I've noticed, as I've gotten older, that I must re-memorize this caution because it's easy to gain speed before you know it.

Checked your gauges lately? Pull up under a streetlight; it will help you to see better.

Yield

"He will be like a tree firmly planted by streams of water, which *yields* its fruit in its season" (Psalm 1:3; italics mine).

I was first drawn to this verse in my early thirties, when I was challenged to find a life verse in Scripture. This one appealed to me because I've always been a bit of a scruffy bush, while this verse challenged me to be a strong tree filled with life-giving fruit and one that offered refuge as well.

Season means (according to the Hebrew diction-ary) "now, certain, continually." That suggests to me that God's trees can always produce. No age restrictions on His grove.

My mom died when she was eighty-seven. To commemorate her life, I planted a Bradford pear tree in my front yard. It fills with blossoms in the spring, greenery in the summer, and flashes of color in the fall, and then it rests during the winter. I watch as birds build nests, hide behind the leaves, and dine on bugs from the bark. It was six feet tall when I planted it, and now it's about fifteen feet. I have a dedicated stream of water on it from our sprinklers and delight in watching it yield to its God-given purpose.

Are you yielding?

Passing Zone

"Then Moses said, 'I pray You, show me Your glory!' And He said, 'I Myself will make all My good-ness *pass* before you'" (Exodus 33:18–19; italics mine).

Sometimes we ask for things that we don't

understand we can't handle. Moses asked to see God's glory, and God replied, "I'll show you my goodness." One of the ways He did that was by covering Moses in the cleft of the rock when He passed by.

Even experiencing God's goodness in a sheltered place left Moses' countenance glowing so bright it frightened the Israelites to the point they were afraid to look at him. They weren't used to streetlights in the desert. Imagine what would have happened had Moses seen God's glory. I personally don't think he would have survived. We're not yet who we will become, and until then, in our fragile earth suits, we can only bear so much of God's fearsome, holy brilliance.

May His goodness pass before you.

Do Not Enter

"He who *does not enter* by the door . . ." (John 10:1; italics mine).

The large-print, clearly lit sign read Do Not Enter. Why does that kind of proclamation breed one's curiosity or at the least become a direct challenge?

Rebellion perhaps? God is very clear: there is only one way into His grace and mercy, and that door is Christ. It is a knee-bending entrance that requires acknowledgment of a power greater than our own.

A friend who had a great fear of death decided as a young woman to check out reincarnation as a possible life option. That door, when opened, led to an endless circle of peaceless existence. Eventually she wobbled her way to the Door of Christ and found His forgiveness, acceptance, and life purpose.

Have you stepped through the well-lit Door? He's waiting.

The way we live our lives has the potential to light paths.

❄

Preach the gospel at all times—if necessary, use words.

—ST. FRANCIS OF ASSISI

fifteen

Spotlight

*There is nothing wrong with change,
if it is in the right direction.*

—WINSTON CHURCHILL

Have you ever grappled? Oh, yeah, that's like asking, "Are you breathing?" Grappling is the sport of life. It's our Olympic high-wire. We grapple with decisions (Should I buy two lipsticks and one purse or two purses and one lipstick?); we grapple with our kids (Roll your eyes at me one more time, and I'll . . .); we grapple with husbands (Roll your eyes at me one more time, and I'll . . .); we grapple with our friends (Roll your eyes . . .). Well, you get the idea. Life involves a lot of eye rolling, as we move from one person to another, one conflict to another, one job to another. We are people in flux.

Flux is continuous change. Hey, girls, that's a great synonym for hormones, don'tcha think? Mine spike about every ten seconds. When I was a young woman, I blamed my crazies on my monthly cycle. Then I shifted into, ahem . . . a more seasoned time in my life, and I blamed my reactionary-self on change of life. Now that I'm just dadgum old, I blame my ornery behavior on my deprived hormones. From now on though, when I act—how shall I say—less than charitable, I will just shout, "Woman in flux! Back away now, and no one will get hurt!"

It really doesn't matter what age we are or what happens to or in our bodies—relationships, jobs, homes, or finances—change is inevitable, and it's jarring when the spotlight of change is aimed in our direction. Flux is the DNA of life. It has the potential to excite us, ignite us, and definitely exhaust us. Too much change at once, and we grapple with security because we base so much of our safety on the known. But the known is flighty and keeps slipping into the hall for a wardrobe change. We are people in transition. And we are people who long for a well-lit path.

If we think about it, life is really one constant transition, as we make our way through this world toward home. At best, life is an awkward suit that, no matter how many times we alter it, it never fits quite right. Oh, we become accustomed to it, even fond of it, but a rustling inside the fabric reminds us this isn't "it"; there's something more . . . much more.

As change hustles us along, we go from the spotlight of kindergarten to caps and gowns, from singleness to marriage, from couplehood to parenthood, from employee to owner, from toddling to doddering, from the work force to retirement.

No wonder we're tired.

Look at the Israelites in Exodus as they joyfully skipped out of Egypt, a change they had longed for, begged for, and prayed for. But instead of the anticipated bliss of the easy life, they ran smack-dab into the Red Sea. (I've hit a few of those myself. Jolting, I must say.) And that was just for openers, with forty years of ongoing change ahead for them. When they did enter their new territory, they found themselves living in the Land of More Transitions.

As do we.

I just moved . . . again. I won't even bore you with my multiple moves, but let me say few, if any, have been my idea. That's not to assign blame, just to suggest that no matter how hard we hold down the brake pedal, change is going to get us, causing us in one way or another to pack up our stuff and move on.

Since change is inevitable, let's look for the best path, lest we wind mindlessly into dry gulches, monotonously circle the desert, or twist endlessly about cavernous tunnels.

Hey, I know! We need a Grappling Position System, a canteen, and a spotlight. My husband was given a two million candlelight–power spotlight. That's what I want. It lights up a half acre of night with one push of the button—that's a big spot.

I'm big on spotlights because I don't deliberately

step into a sea of darkness, nor do I willingly wear blindfolds. I want to see where I'm going, at least to the degree I can, which probably explains why faith has been challenging for me at times.

Les and I grappled with selling our winter getaway in Texas. We initially bought the house because my husband, a heart patient, doesn't do well in cold weather and needs a respite from Michigan's winter. Yet the additional home was an expense that stretched us financially in these changing times. We tried to sell our Michigan home, but the market was sparse, and real estate prices were plummeting; so that wasn't an option. The real estate company held open houses, but no one even walked through. Our downtown had begun to look like a forgotten land with more than twenty empty storefronts as frustrated owners packed up and moved on.

The real estate market was beginning to decline in Texas as well, so we made the decision to put our house on the market to see what would happen. A home down the block had been on the market close to a year with no offers, and we figured it didn't look good for a quick sale for us. In a way we didn't mind because we really loved our place, and we were in no hurry to sell it, even though we knew it was a wise choice.

Grapple, grapple, grapple.

Geri, our Realtor, had a For Sale sign posted in our yard early one evening. The next morning we were surprised to hear that a couple was coming by to look at it and even more surprised when they wrote up an offer that day. We were stunned. I asked my husband, "Does this mean we have to move?" Duh.

The weeks that followed were full of transitioning and grappling. Should we keep the furniture or sell it? Should we buy a condo or rent? Should we drive the car home or shove it in the truck with the couch? (Actually, because it's a PT Cruiser, I could have set it on our couch.)

Some of the best spotlights on truth I've experienced recently are from my friend Jan Silvious, who teaches, "Do what you can and then trust God with the rest." I've found that technique pretty much takes the eye-roll out of grapple and plops us square in the middle of faith. So when I felt overwhelmed with the moving decisions that were coming at me right and left, I engaged in some self-talk. "Self," I said to me, "listen up! Make the smartest choice you know to do and then trust that the God who has been taking care of you since before pabulum will not turn His head now."

Get this: transitions, grappling, flux, DNA, and even hormones are not a disturbance to God. He has a steady plan with our name on it. And a spotlight on that plan.

Whew!

Questions to Ask Yourself

❀ What are you decisive about?

❀ What area of your life is in flux?

❀ What makes you an eye-roller?

❀ What excites you?

❀ Ignites you?

❀ Exhausts you?

Bright Ideas

If I were to turn my husband's spotlight on someone in the Bible who grappled, Gideon would show up in the glare of light. He wrestled with his worth, his calling, and his ability to trust God (Judges 6–7). Yet God chose Gideon to lead His people into and out of war. Amazing.

You would have thought God would have scrutinized Gideon's résumé and considered someone with leadership experience. According to Gideon, he didn't even have potential or desire. In fact, he was hiding when the Lord shone a spotlight on him, calling him to face fierce opponents.

I wonder how many times Gideon rolled his eyes at God's commands before he discovered that with

God on his side he couldn't lose. Now, I must confess, I would have rolled my eyes, too, if God had asked me to fight the well-weaponed enemy with nothing more in my hands than trumpets and pottery. Not conventional, practical, or even reasonable, to say the least. Nonetheless, those were the orders from headquarters. Gideon had to have gone through real change on the inside to risk trusting God with such an unorthodox approach to war: surprise attack (not new); night attack (not new); pots and horns as weaponry (hey, that's unique!).

The night of the attack, Gideon's men blew their trumpets and broke their pitchers, revealing lit torches. The enemy believed, on hearing the shouts and seeing the "spotlights," that they were surrounded, which caused chaos. Then they lashed out at each other, killing many in their own ranks, and finally they ran for their lives.

Who knew?

Only God.

What a bright idea—lit torches inside pitchers. Who would have thought that up?

Only God.

Who knows and spotlights our convoluted life-path with all its successive roundabouts?

Yep.

Only God.

And all God's people said, "Whew!"

❁

Arise, shine, for your light has come,
and the glory of the Lord has risen upon you.

—Isaiah 60:1

sixteen

Lightbulb

> *When Thomas Edison worked late into the night on*
> *the electric light, he had to do it by gas lamp or candle.*
> *I'm sure it made the work seem that much more urgent.*
>
> —GEORGE CARLIN

I remember when lightbulbs were free. Do you? Yes, it definitely dates some of us. Those were the days when all you had to do was bag up your burned-out bulbs and trade them in for new ones. We usually did that one grocery sack full at a time. Whereas today you can invest the price of a pedigree goat or a custom-designed cat into bulb buying just in an attempt to light up the living room.

What's with these new twirly bulbs? Puh-leese, they drive me banana crackers. You know the ones— the longer they're on, the brighter they become, which means you turn them on, and then you must be prepared to wait (like one might for a bus or for freshly painted toenails to dry). I realize these curlicue lightbulbs are "green," and green is in, but give me back my old one-flip-and-I-can-see lightbulbs. By the time the twirlys give me light, I'm done in that room and have moved on. Before I left the room, while I waited for the bulb to "wake up," I had to make my way around by touch and smell, which doesn't work well in the water closet, if you know what I mean.

One of my favorite lightbulbs in the whole house is the one that pops on when I open the refrigerator door. First off, it's not twirly; and second, it instantly illuminates a world of yummy options, even in the middle of the darkest night. Yes!

Refrigerator lights, now that was one bright idea. I love when ideas work. Not all of them do, you know. In fact, the Bible is full of folks who didn't exactly light up their landscape with bright ideas. For instance ...

Sarah's decision to help God out by inviting her husband to sleep with her handmaiden, Hagar, to bear them a child, not only wasn't helpful but also left us still living with the warring repercussions today. Nope, not a bright idea.

Joseph's brothers took sibling rivalry a tad too far. Not good, boys. One should never rub salt in old family wounds. They fester into famines of one kind or another.

King David decided to bypass his kingly duties of going to battle with his men and instead stayed home and was drawn, like one might be to a bath, into the night life. Tsk, tsk, David. You knew better than that.

Samson, oh, Samson, what were you thinking? You knew your girlfriend was in cahoots with your enemies, yet you spilled the beans about your strength. That was a hair-brained idea, if I ever heard one.

Oh, yes, and what about Jonah? He should have invested in a GPS. I'd like to think he forgot which way Nineveh was, but I'm afraid it was just a whale of a bad idea on Jonah's part.

Truth be known, I've been a Sarah at times, trying to help out God. Nope, no handmaidens at our house, I assure you, but my "helpfulness" occurs when I try to control people and alter circumstances. Instead of trusting God's timing and plan, I come up with my own bright ideas, only to have the "bulb" fizzle out.

Joseph's brothers had nothing on me. I confess, as a young woman, I resented that my parents were much more lenient with my little sister than they had been with me. And while, unlike Joseph's brothers, I didn't sell her to a passing caravan, it was only because one didn't come by.

And I'd hate to count the number of times I've ignored my responsibilities. When I was younger, I indulged my emotions and often ignored daily tasks or unpleasant efforts. I still can fall victim to that behavior, if I'm not deliberately attentive to God's ways. King David hasn't cornered the market on irresponsibility, by any means. It's a well-shopped mall.

Hair-brained ideas? If Samson hadn't climbed into the barber's seat, I could have been the mother of that invention. I remember the time I saw a contortionist on TV and thought, *I can do that*. Uh-uh, I was so knotted up I had to call for help to get untied. Duh.

And then there's Nineveh. Who knew, Mr. Jonah, that one wrong turn could leave you with such a sinking feeling? I've made enough wrong turns that I'm still spitting seaweed. Like the time not long ago when I watched a TV show heavy in violence. I knew better, and yet I made that sharp left turn into it. I don't handle hostility well, and I had nightmares for days—actually for nights—afterward.

What I'm trying to say is that we all have allowed our humanity, full of its vices, voices, and violence, to dictate our decisions. God isn't shocked or rocked off His throne by our rebellion, inconsistencies, jealousy, negligence, frailty, fury, or faultiness. He doesn't command us to do certain things, making Him the great dictator in the sky, but He lovingly supplies us with holy boundaries to protect us. God knows the ramifications of our choices, while we are oblivious, deluded, or downright reckless.

As I think about those curlicue lightbulbs, I'm reminded that sometimes it takes awhile for some of us to "wake up." (See that hand in the back of the room? Yes, the woman rubbing her eyes. That would be me.) We're not always our brightest self. It takes time to grow up, wise up, and light up.

Questions to Ask Yourself

- What drives you banana crackers?
- When have you raced ahead of God to help Him out?
- How did that work for you?
- What rivalry resides in your heart? With whom?
- What responsibilities have you been ignoring?
- When was the last time you needed a GPS to stay on course with God's plan for you?

Bright Ideas

I'm a Proverbial girl in that I love the book of Proverbs. I appreciate (usually) how they instantly pop on with a flood of light. One doesn't have to wonder what the writer had in mind. It's right there, in your face.

For instance, try this refrigerator-light proverb: "Put a knife to your throat, if you are a man of great appetite" (Proverbs 23:2).

Yikes! That's startling. Like when you're asleep and some wise guy flips on the overhead lights, it initially blinds you just before it benefits you. Not an easy wake-up call.

Recently I've put on more pounds than I care to own up to, but my clothes, which are no longer covering the acreage, announce that fact loud and clear. So when I read a statement like the above proverb, I'm whiplashed into ownership.

I looked up the word *appetite* from this proverb in a Hebrew dictionary, and it included these defining words: "desire," "discontent," "greedy," "lust," "pleasure." Hmm, I think the ones that illuminated my indulgence the most clearly were "discontent" and "pleasure."

Don't get me wrong. I love my life . . . mostly. But, as with all of us, I have some soul-caustic elements that are hard to bear; so I try to comfort myself with the pleasure of food.

The funny thing about overindulgence is that, while it's happening, it's a pleasure. But afterward, it's a dark, one-way elevator shaft . . . down.

I love pasta, pies, and puddings (flan, custard, crème brûlée). I also am gaga over thick bread slathered in butter. Yes, real butter. And I'm a big proponent of ordering a plethora of desserts after a meal to try them all. Yes, that's greedy. I know, I know.

I've been asking myself, "Why are you eating like this, and why don't you stop?"

Self didn't respond—too busy chewing. So I've been asking the Lord in prayer to reveal to me what's going on, and the thought that has flooded my mind is that I'm running to food to soothe my angst rather than running to Christ.

Food never has resolved my issues beyond filling my stomach and padding my waistline, so why would I do that? Well, food has immediate availability, and I've noticed that God often takes His time. Also, in my humanity, I'm self-destructive. Only when I set my mind on spirit matters am I led into life and peace. Notice the word *led*, which denotes a journey, and that suggests time. I like microwave answers. Hurry is my lifestyle.

So it's back to the drawing board and the calorie counting. I don't want to finish my race full of guilt and bulging with greed. Besides, it's hard to run while carrying the weight of bad choices.

While a dessert fest sounds like a bright idea . . . it isn't.

❀

For those who are according to the flesh set their minds on the things of the flesh, but those who are according to the Spirit, the things of the Spirit.

—ROMANS 8:5

seventeen

Lighthouse

> *We are told to let our light shine, and if it does, we won't
> need to tell anybody it does. Lighthouses don't fire cannons
> to call attention to their shining—they just shine.*
>
> —DWIGHT L. MOODY

I've known a plethora of lighthouses . . . walking,
talking, bona fide lit towers who, at critical moments, through tumultuous waters, have guided
me and others to shore.

My mom was what you would call a short stack.
She was a four feet ten inches tower beaconing me
home. Not just to our house but also to the city we
seek. Her methodology is worth considering, for
Mom not only blinked a bright light so I could find

her in the dark, but she also would wade into the deep and help to tow me in. It was her way.

God bless the heart God gives to mothers who, at any price, will do what they can to help their children find their bearings: through the fog, through the flood, through the storm, through the darkness . . . *through* is the operative word. Mom demonstrated that, together, we would make it through.

If Mom had known her only son would fall asleep at the wheel of his car, she would have gladly taken his place. By the time I found out about my brother's accident and made my way to the hospital, the prognosis was bleak. On hearing the news, a blood vessel in Mom's eye burst, leaving it blood red, and her back slipped out of place, leaving her with a limp. It is a violent act to tell a mother her child will not live, regardless of that child's age.

The dark waters of grief covered my mother and threatened her existence, until with time, faith swirled, and she rose up into a new light—first a flicker and then a flood. I have seen with my eyes that mothers whose children have died no longer fear death. The sting has been removed, and heaven becomes for them a closer shore, a sweeter land.

Several years ago in the land of lakes, Minnesota, I spotted a tall, lit tower by the name of Mary Jo. Mary Jo is a lighthouse marvel. She has Lou Gehrig's, amyotrophic degenerative, disease. (*A-myo-trophic* comes from the Greek. *A-* means "no." *Myo-* refers to muscle, and *trophic* means "nourishment": no muscle nourishment.)

Mary Jo can't talk because her vocal cords are paralyzed, but mind you, she says volumes. Her bright, dark eyes flash with passion, pleasure, purpose, and at times sadness. When I met her, it wasn't at her home or at the hospital, but in a most unexpected place. At a Women of Faith conference, amid a sea of thousands of women, I first witnessed her light. Her daughter, Sarah, invited me to step into the radiance of her mom. Obviously Sarah was proud of her.

When I walked down to greet Mary Jo, I was stunned. How could this be? Why, this woman was critically ill and required many attendants to care for her, and yet there she was in a specially designed wheelchair with tubes discreetly taking care of her most intimate needs. At first I thought how heroic her friends were to bring her, but I was to learn it was Lighthouse Mary Jo who had brought them.

After our first meeting, I didn't expect to see Mary Jo again. I thought surely she wouldn't live to attend the following year's conference. Yet, year after year her light continues to reach across the rugged waves of her life, giving hope to others, and year after year she attends yet another conference with her entourage and medical team.

I asked Sarah if her mom ever went anywhere else, and I was surprised to hear Mary Jo is a busy mom who attends all her son's sporting events. Hello! This woman has to be fed with a feeding tube, and she goes on outings to support her children? (Excuse me, but I'm embarrassed for my lame excuses.)

Who would blame Mary Jo if she didn't leave home? It's risky, to say the least. And get this: she makes up the menus for the family every week, even though she'll never taste even a mouthful. She constructs honey-do lists for her husband of things that need to be taken care of around the house. Most folks bail on the daily tasks when they are fighting for their lives, but not this Lighthouse. And her son is known to check with Mom for permission before be-bopping out the door and to report to her on his homework and grades. Talk about being in the moment and fully engaged.

Mary Jo sent me a thank-you note. Me. How humbling. I knew what an effort that note was because she can't use her hands or arms, but she has a muscle behind her leg that she can move against a button, while seated in a chair, that's connected to the computer. Laboriously she flinches that muscle to strike one letter at a time until her message is complete. T-h-a-n-k Y-o-u.

Don't you think she's brave? Don't you think she's bright? She's a spectacular lighthouse. With the muscle in her lifted eyebrows, Mary Jo spells words, and with her lifted faith she sends a clear message—not SOS, but "This little light of mine, I'm going to let it shine."

QUESTIONS TO ASK YOURSELF

❀ Who make up the plethora of lighthouses in your life?

❀ Who has "towed" you in? When?

❀ When was the last time you were aware of faith swirling up inside you?

❀ What area of your life needs nourishment?

❀ What makes your eyes flash with passion? pleasure? purpose?

❀ Who do you need to thank? What will it cost you?

BRIGHT IDEAS

Two lighthouses aligned—one taller, one shorter—are said to form a "range," used to help ships navigate tricky waterways and dark coastlines.

Scripture tells us that where two or three

believers are aligned in agreement, Christ is in the midst of them. Christ loves when we come together in harmony and in the best interest of others. His whole ministry was an outreach to others. He taught the sinking Peter who it was that could lift him out of deep waters. He taught a shipful of frightened disciples that no storm could overtake them if He who created the sea and stirred the waves was in their midst.

The book of Ecclesiastes tells us that a threefold cord is not easily broken (4:12) and that two are better than one (4:9). The theme is repeated throughout Scripture to remind us that not only were we meant to connect our faith but also that it makes us stronger, brighter, and more able to toss a lifeline to others.

Several years ago, our family went through a heartbreaking, life-crippling crisis. We quickly pulled together, linked arms, and helped to shore each other up as wave after wave slammed against us. But one night, when my family wasn't near, unexpected waves of grief blindsided me.

Gratefully God has given us the family of God,

and a "sister" saw me sinking into the darkness and threw out the lifeline of prayer. She was at my knees within seconds of my descent, beseeching God on my behalf, and no sooner did her knees touch the floor than four other "sisters" aligned in agreement with her. From one moment to the next I have never felt such wildly opposing feelings: debilitating, dark despair and then the life-giving light of hope.

That's what it's all about, girlfriend. Christ gave His life for us as a sacrifice and as a reminder that we're called to sacrificially give ourselves for others. We become lighthouses powered by the hope we have in Christ. We have the responsibility and joy of standing tall and shining bright—with all of our heart, soul, and strength, right down to our last moments and our last flinching muscle flashing out—for others on dark seas, our gratitude.

T-h-a-n-k Y-o-u.

❈

Darkness reigns at the foot of the lighthouse.

—JAPANESE PROVERB

eighteen

Let There Be Light

I have a jazzy new silver jacket. Think tinfoil. Shiny tinfoil. I'm teased by friends who have varying opinions of what I look like in it. A hubcap, a rocket ship, a tuna fish can, and a baked potato have been offered as options.

Even with that many choices, I couldn't decide which was more accurate. Okay, maybe the hubcap, because I run around in circles a lot. Although I've gained weight recently so I could be an aluminum-wrapped, chubby baked potato. Hey, better yet, maybe I look like a foil-wrapped Hershey's Kiss. Okay, maybe not.

I was drawn to the jacket because it's reflective; light bounces off it in all directions. It reminds me of friendship. I think friendships are reflective, don't you? At least good ones. Friends help us to capture reflections of ourselves that we might otherwise miss. And because iron sharpens iron (or tinfoil buffs tinfoil), those reflections are heightened.

Do you think fifty years is a long time? I do. In fact, I think most folks would agree, since the estimated average length of a life isn't much longer than that. Well, fifty years is how long Carol Porter and I have been friends. That's a lot of calendar pages and tons of reflective memories.

Our lives are inextricably laced with threads of celebration and heartache. We grew up together through junior high and high school, spending many nights at each other's homes. We danced until we were breathless, and we double-dated. We were well acquainted with each other's parents and siblings. We vacationed together, including the trip on which I met my husband. Today our husbands are buddies, and we've watched each other's children grow up and cradle their own babies. Carol painted wall murals throughout my home. I did the eulogy at her youngest son's funeral. When you span that many years, you can't help but know a great deal about each other. Information that goes way past, "What's your favorite color?"

Our birthdays are ten days apart. When we were young, those ten days were significant. Now, not so much.

Carol makes an appearance in every book I've written, with the exception of my children's books. Two of the books were dedicated to her. She did the artwork in three of my books, and photographs of her appear in my books about tea and about home.

I tell you all this so you will understand the depth of my heartache when Carol was diagnosed with breast cancer. It frightened us, but the doctors quickly moved forward with surgery. Then she had treatments, and her hair fell out. She was unusually brave and grew stronger through the process.

Good news came when the doctor gave her the all clear. We celebrated. Her hair grew back. She and Bruce traveled to Europe. Life was back on track. And then ...

I was at a Women of Faith conference when word reached me that Carol was back in the hospital, the cancer was rampant, and she wasn't doing well. I left the conference as soon as I could to race to her bedside. She looked fragile and frightened. We learned soon after that the cancer was in her shoulder, her lung, and her liver.

The news took Carol's breath away. We who love her struggled for our composure. She grew downcast and quiet, which deeply concerned me. I wanted to fix her, like when we were kids. If she was afraid, I would protect her and then make her laugh. If anyone even thought of picking on her, I rose up as defender.

As a kid, Carol was reticent, shy, quiet, and fearful. I saved up my fear until adulthood, when I became agoraphobic, but as a kid I was bold and sassy. Today, as a senior, I'm once again feisty, but feisty doesn't fix what Carol has. It won't put hair on her bald head, make her recurring hives disappear, give her back her voice (affected by a paralyzed vocal cord), or chase her cancer back to hell. I would fix it all if I could.

After hearing the palpable sadness in Carol's voice during a phone visit one evening, after I hung up, I felt especially helpless. I cried out to the Lord for guidance. I wanted to say something to help her, but I was powerless and wordless, two very empty places to be.

During my prayer, I reminded the Lord that I had a sporadic history of saying the wrong thing. I didn't want to make that mistake with my dear, vulnerable friend. "Lord, please give me guidance from Your Word. I want to give Carol something from Your counsel that will go deep inside her, into the very marrow of her bones. Something that will help pull her out of this sad funk she's in."

As I scanned Scripture, looking for a verse or chapter I could offer, I felt no prompting from God's Spirit. Then, as I prayed again, these words flooded into my heart: *"Let there be light."*

That didn't make sense to me. "Let there be light" is my morning verse, not a word for someone as sick as Carol. So I suggested to the Lord that the psalms had a long history of comforting people and that maybe one of them might be the right prescription for a heartsick friend.

"*Let there be light*" flooded my heart again.

Still I resisted. "What about the Gospels, Lord?"

Silence.

Then the words tumbled back inside of me. "*Let there be light.*"

I can't tell you how awkward I felt about going to my dearest friend and saying, "Let there be light."

In the book of Job the question is posed, "Who would counsel the Lord?" I realized how ludicrous it was to try to tell God His business. Yet I struggled with the sack lunch He had packed for me to offer Carol.

I should have known He had blessed it first.

When I called Carol and told her the verse, she was as reluctant to receive it as I had been to offer it.

I said, "Well, when we think about it, those are

the first recorded words we have from God, and the Bible does open with light, closes with a reference to light, and in between focuses on Jesus, the Light of the World. So perhaps you could offer the words as a prayer. Just every time you think of it say, 'Let there be light.'"

Carol agreed to do that, but with forced enthusiasm. She wanted more, and I wanted to offer her more. We both wanted something that fell instantly on her spirit with healing and billowed up with comfort.

About a week and a half later, Carol called me about a doctor's appointment she had the day before. Her voice was jubilant. My heart leaped at the new energy in her voice.

"Patsy, wait until I tell you what happened. It didn't hit me until three o'clock this morning when I sat bolt upright in bed. I went to the doctor's yesterday to hear what he had found in my bone scan. It wasn't good," she reported. "He began to tell me all the places the cancer had spread in my bones. I could feel my spirit dip; so I stopped listening.

That's why, when he said what he did, it didn't sink in until the middle of the night."

"Oh, Carol, hurry; tell me, what did he say?"

"He told me that he was looking for flashes of light in the scan because those places denote that my antibodies are destroying the cancer."

Then Carol proclaimed, "Oh, Patsy, I've been praying, 'Let there be light,' and it was the very thing I needed most! I got so excited I even woke up my husband to tell him. I couldn't wait."

As I listened, I was jumping up and down, clapping as the realization flooded over me. I had asked for words that would go into the marrow of my friend's bones figuratively, and God had given them in reality!

Initially, I was disappointed that the Lord hadn't led me to obvious passages of comfort for Carol. Little did I realize that He had given powerful words of healing.

Even during that happy phone call, Carol was aware she hadn't been totally restored, but God had given her words of life. The personalization of that truth caused a surge of joy to permeate her.

Since that loving reminder of God's personal involvement in Carol's journey, we have spoken often of the verse, and we both continue to pray it. Recently Carol's liver showed the first signs of shutting down. That was a terrible jolt. But then, after a round of a radical chemo-cocktail, the swelling in her liver reduced, and the liver began to work again.

Carol and I talk about how precious our numbered days are, the importance of embracing each one as a gift and of treasuring those whom we love. Yesterday I interviewed her, gathering heart information about her life, just as a way to treasure her and our time together. Most of the questions I asked I already knew the answers to because we've shared our lives since childhood, but she surprised me with a few stories I had never heard before. The remembrances of years gone by stirred many feelings in us both.

The doctors have begun to speak of hospice care for my friend. She is adjusting to that offer, and I wouldn't be surprised if in the near future she chooses that route. If she has a few steps left or many, I call myself fortunate to take them with her as far as I'm allowed. And if she leaves ahead of me, I shall miss her deeply. Yet because she is firmly stitched inside my heart, she'll always remain a significant contributor to my life. And one day, one glorious day, we will celebrate the Light together.

So while "Let there be light" felt like I was offering my friend a firefly when she needed a galaxy of supernovas, it contained power I never would have suspected. With that very statement, God began the creation of all we know, as He harnessed darkness into night as light ripped through to declare day. And if that wasn't enough, God placed light holders into the night sky so we would be reminded we're never alone, a sweet thought when my dear friend is leaning heavenward.

I've learned that pain can isolate us and cause us to feel alone in our journey, even when we have those around us who care. But a word from the Lord companions us as nothing else can . . . because it goes into the very marrow of our existence.

I'm surprised at how small my vision is for God. I've walked and talked with Him for years, and yet I'm still startled by His generosity and jolted by His desire to know us and to be known by us. To remind us of that, throughout the universe, He has dispersed light to give us life, insight, direction, protection, and hope, that we might consider Him and His ways . . . from a glorious dawn to the setting sun, from a diamond-studded night to a full-faced moon, from a slash of lightning to the sparkling backside of a gyrating firefly.

Listen, why don't you go get that dusty blue mason jar out of your garage, poke holes in the lid, and tonight capture some shimmering moon beams, a sprinkling of stardust, and a few flickering fireflies?

Whatever you do . . . don't miss the show.

Let there be light!